165.0
30

Alcoholic Korsakoff's Syndrome
AN INFORMATION-PROCESSING APPROACH TO AMNESIA

Alcoholic Korsakoff's Syndrome

AN INFORMATION-PROCESSING APPROACH TO AMNESIA

Nelson Butters
Laird S. Cermak

Psychology Service
Veterans Administration Medical Center
and
Neurology Department
Boston University School of Medicine
Boston, Massachusetts

1980

ACADEMIC PRESS

A Subsidiary of Harcourt Brace Jovanovich, Publishers

New York   London   Toronto   Sydney   San Francisco

ACADEMIC PRESS, INC.
111 Fifth Avenue, New York, New York 10003

United Kingdom Edition published by
ACADEMIC PRESS, INC. (LONDON) LTD.
24/28 Oval Road, London NW1   7DX

Library of Congress Cataloging in Publication Data

Butters, Nelson.
    Alcoholic Korsakoff's syndrome.

    Includes bibliographical references and index.
    1.   Korsakoff's syndrome.   I.   Cermak, Laird S. ,
joint author.   II.   Title.   [DNLM: 1.   Amnesia——
Etiology. 2.   Korsakoff's syndrome.   WM173.7 B988a]
RC394.K6B8   616.85'232   79—6779
ISBN 0—12—148380—0

To Arlene, Meryl, Paul, and Lisa
for their love and encouragement.
—N. B.

Dedicated with lasting love
to my wife Sharon and daughter Kendra
and to Shawn Brendan whose life, although brief,
will remain in our thoughts forever.
—L. S. C.

Contents

CONTENTS

Preface

The amount of investigation of the amnesic component of Korsakoff's syndrome has increased considerably during the past decade and a half. Stimulated primarily by Talland's (1965) *Deranged Memory,* Victor, Adams, and Collins's (1971) treatise on *The Wernicke Korsakoff Syndrome,* and Milner's work on hippocampectomized patients, investigators from diverse areas of expertise have focused on this problem in recent years. Perhaps most active in investigating this area have been the neuropsychologists. But their investigations of amnesia have not been without controversy and, indeed, several theories have emerged to explain all or parts of the syndrome. These theoretical approaches have sometimes conflicted, sometimes complemented one another. But, throughout, they have created an environment that stimulates research and draws new investigators into the field in rapidly burgeoning numbers. This has made the study of amnesia one of the most exciting areas of investigation, not only within neuropsychology, but within psychology in general.

The primary purpose of this book is to present an overview of one of these theories of amnesia, namely, the extent to which it represents an information-processing deficit. This focus is not meant to ignore other theories and interpretations. In fact, wherever possible, we have tried to show how the data emanating from other viewpoints might fit into a "processing-deficits" framework, and we have contrasted other theoretical approaches to the major theme of this book. We do not wish to imply that our theoretical position is the only stance that should be taken. Rather, this book has been written to present a more concise and comprehensive overview of the "information-processing deficits" theory of amnesia.

The joint research program we designed to assess the extent of information-processing deficits in alcoholic Korsakoff patients began about 1972 when we found a large area of overlap between Butters' interest in the neuropsychology of amnesia and Cermak's interest in memory processes. Since that time we have continuously melded these two areas of interest through daily consultation and discussion. As a consequence, our present thinking, we believe, encompasses the most current theorizing within each discipline and continually seeks to incorporate both into our overall program. That this combining of knowledge has been productive is evidenced primarily by the publication of this book.

Naturally, both our research program and the undertaking of the writing of this book would not have been accomplished without the support and efforts of others. We have been supported financially by the National Institute of Alcohol and Alcohol Abuse (NIAAA) through Grant No. AA00187 to Boston University School of Medicine and funds from the Medical Research Service of the Veterans Administration. Numerous colleagues, collaborators, and research assistants have aided in the collection, tabulation, and interpretation of data over the years. Much of their efforts are cited throughout this text. We are particularly indebted, however, to Dr. Harold Goodglass, Director of Psychology Research, for his support and supervision, to Dr. Ralph Fingar, Chief of Psychology, and to the entire Psychology Service at the Boston Veterans Administration Medical Center. Special appreciation is extended to Barbara Uhly, Kathy Montgomery, and Mary Cambell for their help in editing this book; and to Betty Norky, Nancy Hatley, Claire Sybertz, and Sharon Barry for typing various drafts of the manuscript.

Acknowledgments

We are grateful to the following for permission to use the figures and tables indicated.

Figure 1.1, 10.4, 10.5, and 10.6 (pp. 3, 164, 165, and 166): From Ryan, C., Butters, N., Montgomery, K., Adinolfi, B., and Didario, B., Memory deficits in chronic alcoholics: Continuities between the "intact" alcoholic and the alcoholic Korsakoff patient, in H. Begleiter and B. Kissin (Eds.), *Alcohol intoxification and withdrawal*, New York Plenum, 1979, Figures 3, 5, 6, and 7;

Figures 1.2 and 1.3 (pp. 6 and 7): From Albert, M., Butters, N., and Levin, J., Temporal gradients in the retrograde amnesia of patients with alcoholic Korsakoff's syndrome, *Archives of Neurology*, 1979, *36*, 211–216, Figures 2 and 3, Copyright 1979, American Medical Association.

Figures 1.2, 1.3, 1.4, 6.7, 6.9, 8.2, 8.4, and 8.7 (pp. 6, 7, 9, 107, 108, 127, 134, and 138): From Heilman, K. M., and Valenstein, E., *Clinical neuropsychology*, New York, Oxford University Press, 1979, Figures 1–3, 5 and 7–11.

Figures, 3.1, 4.4, 4.5, and 4.6 (pp. 35, 55, 56, and 57): From Cermak, L. S., Butters, N., and Goodglass, H., The extent of memory loss in Korsakoff patients, *Neuropsychologia*, 1971, *9*, 307–315, Figures 1, 2, 3, and 6.

Figures 3.3, 4.1, 4.2, and 4.3 (pp. 39, 51, 52, and 54): From Baddeley, A. D., and Warrington, E. K., Amnesia and the distinction between long- and short-term memory, *Journal of Verbal Learning and Verbal Behavior*, 1970, *9*, 176–189, Figures 1, 2, and 3.

Figures 3.4 and 4.7 (pp. 40 and 58): From Cermak, L. S., and Butters, N., The role of interference and encoding in the short-term memory deficits of Korsakoff patients, *Neuropsychologia,* 1972, *10,* 89–96, Figures 1 and 3.

Figures 3.5, 3.6, and 3.7 (pp. 41 and 42): From Cermak, L. S., Naus, M. J., and Reale, L., Rehearsal strategies of alcoholic Korsakoff patients, *Brain and Language,* 1976, *3,* 375–385, Figures 1, 2, and 3.

Figure 4.8 (p. 60): From DeLuca, D., Cermak, L. S., and Butters, N., The differential effects of semantic, acoustic, and nonverbal distraction on Korsakoff patients' verbal retention performance, *International Journal of Neuroscience,* 1976, *6,* 279–284, Figure 2.

Figure 4.9 (p. 61): From Cermak, L. S., Reale, L., and DeLuca, D., Korsakoff patients' nonverbal versus verbal memory: Effects of interference and mediation on rate of information loss, *Neuropsychologia,* 1977, *15,* 303–310, Figure 1.

Figure 4.10 (p. 63): From Butters, N. and Grady, M., Effect of predistractor delays on the short-term memory performance of patients with Korsakoff's and Huntington's disease, *Neuropsychologia,* 1977, *15,* 701–706, Figure 1, Copyright 1977, Pergamon Press, Ltd.

Figure 4.11 (p. 67): From Cermak, L. S., and Uhly, B., Short-term motor memory in Korsakoff patients, *Perceptual and Motor Skills,* 1975, *40,* 278, Figure 1.

Figures 5.1 and 5.2 (pp. 73 and 75): From Cermak, L. S., Butters, N., and Gerrein, J., The extent of the verbal encoding ability of Korsakoff patients, *Neuropsychologia,* 1973, *11,* 85–94, Figures 1 and 2.

Figure 5.3 (p. 78): From Cermak, L. S., and Moreines, J., Verbal retention deficits in aphasic and amnesic patients, *Brain and Language,* 1976, *3,* 16–27, Figure 5.

Figures 5.4, 5.5, 5.6, and 5.7 (pp. 80, 81, and 82): From Cermak, L. S., Butters, N., and Moreines, J., Some analyses of the verbal encoding deficit of alcoholic Korsakoff patients, *Brain and Language,* 1974, *1,* 141–150, Figures 1–4.

Figure 6.1 (p. 97): From Glosser, G., Butters, N., and Kaplan, E. Visuoperceptual processes in brain damaged patients on the digit symbol substitution test, *International Journal of Neuroscience,* 1977, 7, 59–66, Figure 1.

Figures 6.5 and 6.6 (pp. 102 and 103): From Kapur, N., and Butters, N., Visuoperceptive deficits in long-term alcoholics and alcoholics with Korsakoff's psychosis, *Journal of Studies on Alcohol,* 1977, *38,* 2025–2035, Figures 1 and 2, Copyright by Journal of Studies on Alcohol, Inc., New Brunswick, N.J. 08903.

Figures 6.7, 6.8, and 6.9 (pp. 107 and 108): From Dricker, J., Butters,

N., Berman, G., Samuels, I., and Carey, S., Recognition and encoding of faces by alcoholic Korsakoff and right hemisphere patients, *Neuropsychologia*, 1978, *16*, 683–695, Figures 1, 2, and 3, Copyright 1978, Pergamon Press, Ltd.

Table 7.1 (p. 115): From Warrington, E., and Weiskrantz, L., Amnesic syndrome: Consolidation or retrieval? *Nature*, 1970, *228*, 628–630, Table 3.

Figures 8.1 and 8.6 (pp. 126 and 136): From Goldstein, G., and Neuringer, C. (Eds.), *Empirical studies of alcoholism*, 1976, Cambridge, Mass., Ballinger, Figures 6.15 and 6.19, Copyright 1976, Ballinger Publishing Company.

Figures 8.3 and 8.5 (pp. 133 and 135): From Butters, N., Tarlow, S., Cermak, L. S., and Sax, D., A comparison of the information processing deficits of patients with Huntington's Chorea or Korsakoff's syndrome, *Cortex*, 1976, *xii*, 134–144, Figures 1 and 4.

Figure 8.8 (p. 139): From Butters, N., Albert, M., and Sax, D., Some investigations of patients with Huntington's disease, In Chase, T., Barbeau, A., and Wexler, N., *Huntington's Chorea: 1972–1978*, New York, Raven Press, Figures 4 and 5.

Figure 9.1 (p. 145): From Jones, B. P., Moskowitz, H. R., and Butters, N., Olfactory discrimination in alcoholic Korsakoff patients, *Neuropsychologia*, 1975, *13*, 173–179, Figure 2, Copyright 1975, Pergamon Press, Ltd.

Figures 9.2, 9.3, and 9.4 (pp. 146 and 147): Jones, B. P., Moscowitz, H. R., Butters, N., and Glosser, G., Psychophysical scaling of olfactory, visual, and auditory stimuli by alcoholic Korsakoff patients, *Neuropsychologia* 1975, *13*, 387–393, Figures 1, 2, and 3, Copyright 1975, Pergamon Press, Ltd.

Figures 9.5, 9.6, 9.7, 9.8, and 9.9 (pp. 151, 152, 153, and 154): From Jones, B. P., Butters, N., Moskowitz, H. R., and Montgomery, K., Olfactory and gustatory capacities of alcoholic Korsakoff patients, *Neuropsychologia*, 1978, *16*, 323–327, Figures 1, 2, 3, 5, and 6, Copyright 1978, Pergamon Press, Ltd.

Figures 10.1, 10.2, and 10.3 (pp. 159, 160, and 161): From Butters, N., Cermak, L. S., Montgomery, K. M., and Adinolfi, A., Some comparisons of the memory and visuoperceptive deficits of chronic alcoholics and patients with Korsakoff's disease, *Alcoholism: Clinical and Experimental Research*, 1977, *1*, 73–80, Figures 1, 3, 6.

Figure 10.7 (p. 168): From Albert, M., Butters, N., and Levin, J., Memory for remote events in chronic alcoholics and alcoholic Korsakoff patients. In H. Begleiter and B. Kissin (Eds.), *Biological effects of alcohol,* New York, Plenum, 1980, Figures 2 and 4.

Figure 2.2 (p. 26): From Sperling, G., The information available in brief visual presentations, *Psychological Monographs,* 1960, *74,* Whole No. 498. Copyright 1960 by the American Psychological Association. Reprinted by permission.

Figure 2.1 (p. 22): From Peterson, L. R., and Peterson, M. J., Short-term retention of individual items, *Journal of Experimental Psychology,* 1959, *58,* 193–198. Copyright 1959 by the American Psychological Association. Reprinted by permission.

Figures 5.8–5.14 (pp. 85, 86, 88, 89, and 90): From Cermak, L. S., and Reale, L., Depth of processing and retention of words by alcoholic Korsakoff patients, *Journal of Experimental Psychology,* 1978, *4,* 165–174. Copyright 1978 by the American Psychologcial Association. Reprinted by permission.

Alcoholic Korsakoff's Syndrome
AN INFORMATION-PROCESSING APPROACH TO AMNESIA

1

Clinical Symptoms, Neuropathology, and Etiology

In 1881, Carl Wernicke described a neurological syndrome in three patients (two male alcoholics, one woman with sulfuric acid poisoning) that included ataxia, optic abnormalities, and a confusional state. Postmortem examination of these three patients showed small punctate hemorrhages that were symmetrically located in the gray matter around the third and fourth ventricles of their brains. Wernicke characterized these findings, which now bears his name, as an acute inflammatory disease of the ocular–motor nuclei, and noted that the symptoms were progressive and led to death in approximately 2 weeks. Six years following the publication of Wernicke's paper, S. S. Korsakoff published the first of a series of reports in which he detailed the amnesic and confabulatory symptoms that often accompanied disorders involving polyneuropathy. Although long-term alcoholism often preceded these mental changes, Korsakoff noted that the symptoms also followed a number of other conditions, such as persistent vomiting, typhoid fever, and intestinal obstruction. On the basis of his observations, he concluded that the presence of a substance toxic to the peripheral and central nervous systems must have been the common denominator in his reported cases. Although neither Wernicke nor Korsakoff could be specific with regard to etiology, and both seemed unaware that their two syndromes often occurred sequentially in the same patients, their clinical descriptions of the symptomatology were accurate and represented important initial steps in the identification and understanding of the Wernicke-Korsakoff syndrome.

The major symptoms of the Wernicke stage include a global confusional state, opthalmoplegia, nystagmus, ataxia, and a polyneuropathy (e.g., pain, loss of sensation, weakness) of the legs and arms. Of these neurological symptoms, the global confusional state is perhaps most germane to our interests. The patient is disoriented regarding time and place, is unable to recognize familiar people, is apathetic, inattentive, and, most significantly, is unable to maintain a coherent conversation. It is important to note that this confusional state makes assessment of memory during the Wernicke phase of an illness both difficult and of questionable validity. Memory capacities can only be assessed if it is certain that the material to be learned is attended to and comprehended, and such certainties cannot be guaranteed during the Wernicke phase of an illness. Thus, all the neuropsychological assessments described in the following chapters were conducted when the patients had passed into the chronic Korsakoff stage of their illness.

If patients with Wernicke encephalopathies are not treated with large doses of thiamine, they are in danger of having fatal midbrain hemorrhages. If, however, patients receive proper vitamin therapy, their neurological symptoms will evidence marked improvement. In most cases, the ocular problems will almost disappear, the ataxia and peripheral neuropathies will improve, and the confusional state will clear. That is, after 2 or 3 weeks of thiamine treatment, patients will realize that they are in a hospital, recognize their spouse and children, and be able to maintain an intelligible conversation with their physicians. At this point, the patients have passed the acute Wernicke phase and have entered the chronic Korsakoff stage. Very few patients in the Wernicke phase show a complete recovery to their premorbid intellectual state.

The Korsakoff patients' *anterograde amnesia* is the most striking feature of their disorder. They are unable to learn new verbal and nonverbal information from the time of the onset of their illness. Learning the name of their physician, nurses, the name of the hospital, and even the location of their bed, may require weeks or months of constant repetition and rehearsal. Events that occurred hours or even minutes before will be lost to the amnesic individual. Not only do they fail to learn the names of important people and places, but often they will not remember previous encounters with these individuals. If the patients spend 3 hours completing a number of psychometric tasks, they will fail to recall the entire test session 2 hours after it has ended. Three common words read to the patient cannot be recalled 10 sec later. As one of our patients described his existence, "I always feel as though I am just waking up. I don't remember what happened a minute ago. I don't know the meaning of what's going on." Experimentally, this severe anterograde problem is exemplified by the severe difficulty the Korsakoff patient has in learning even short lists of five or six paired-associates. When alcoholic Korsakoff patients are shown a list of word pairs (e.g., man–hammer) in which they must learn to associate the second word with the first, the acquisition of these associations may require 70 or 80 trials instead of the three or four presentations needed by intact subjects.

Figure 1.1 presents the results of a verbal, paired-associate learning task in which alcoholic Korsakoff patients, long-term alcoholics, and intact normal control subjects (with all groups carefully matched for age and educational background) attempted to learn a list of 10 word-pairs (Ryan, Butters, Montgomery, Adinolfi, & Didario, 1980). Although the long-term alcoholic results are inferior to those of the normal control group, both groups evidence considerable learning over the eight test trials. In fact, most of the normal controls acquire the entire 10 word-pairs by the eighth trial. The alcoholic Korsakoff patients, however, demonstrate virtually no learning during the eight trials. Their performance on Trials 7 and 8 shows little improvement

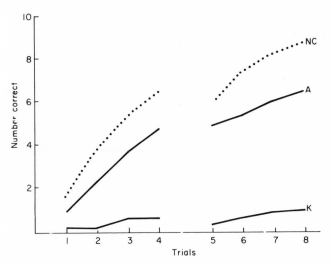

FIGURE 1.1 *The diagram compares the mean number of words recalled on a verbal paired-associate task for normal controls (NC), alcoholics (A), Korsakoff alcoholics (K).*

over Trials 1 and 2. Such failures to learn new materials are the rule for alcoholic Korsakoff patients and remain the most obvious symptom of Korsakoff's syndrome.

Retrograde amnesia is also a distinct and consistent feature of Korsakoff's syndrome. The patient has trouble retrieving from long-term memory events that occurred prior to the onset of the illness. When asked who was President of the United States before Mr. Nixon, the patient might answer "Truman" or "Eisenhower." In 1975, we asked one of our then recently diagnosed Korsakoff patients if the United States was still at war. The patient replied, "I think they have that war in Korea all wrapped up." In general, this difficulty in retrieving old memories is usually more pronounced for events just prior to the onset of the illness, whereas remote events from the patient's childhood and early adulthood are well remembered. Most Korsakoff patients who served in World War II can describe their tours of duty with great detail and apparent accuracy but are unable to recall any of the major historical events of the 1960s (e.g., the assassination of the Kennedy brothers, Vietnam War protests).

This temporal "gradient" is not only evident during a mental status examination but has been demonstrated in numerous experimental studies. Seltzer and Benson (1974) used a multiple choice questionnaire and found that their alcoholic Korsakoff patients could remember famous events from the 1930s and 1940s better than events from the 1960s and 1970s. Marslen-Wilson and Teuber (1975) presented alcoholic Korsakoff patients with photographs of famous people and found that the patients had much more difficulty identifying famous faces from the 1960s than faces from the 1930s and 1940s.

Warrington and her associates have challenged the existence of this gradient and have presented evidence that amnesic patients have as much difficulty retrieving remote (e.g., childhood) events as recent events. Sanders and Warrington (1971) administered a "famous events" questionnaire and a test of famous faces to five amnesics (mixed etiology). Their patients were impaired relative to the control group on all tests and for all periods of time. Unlike the impairment observed in the studies just reviewed, these patients' impairment was of equal severity at all time periods. Warrington believes that the difference between her results and those of other studies is related to the relative difficulty of the test items. That is, although Warrington attempted to insure that items from different decades were of equal difficulty (i.e., she chose people and events whose fame did not ex-

4

tend beyond a single decade), such controls were not evident in other studies of retrograde amnesia. According to Warrington, it is entirely possible that the temporal gradients described by other investigators (Marslen-Wilson & Teuber, 1975; Seltzer & Benson, 1974) may be due to the fact that questions and faces from the 1930s and 1940s were easier to answer or recognize than those from the 1960s and 1970s. Warrington feels that if one insures that all questions are of equal difficulty, then the "gradient" of retrograde amnesia disappears, and the patient shows equal difficulty in recalling remote and recent past events. In Chapter 7 we shall see that this "flat" retrograde amnesia is one of the cornerstones of Warrington's retrieval theory of amnesia.

Albert, Butters, and Levin (1979) have reexamined retrograde amnesia in light of Warrington's criticisms of other studies. Three tests were developed: a famous faces test, a recall questionnaire, and a multiple-choice recognition questionnaire. Each test consisted of items from the 1920s to the 1970s that had been assessed with a sizeable population of normal controls before their inclusion in the final test battery. Half the items were "easy," as judged by the performance of the standardization group; the other half were difficult or "hard," as judged by the same criterion. All the easy items concerned people or events whose fame spanned many decades (e.g., Charlie Chaplin, Charles Lindburgh), and the hard items, people or events whose fame were limited to one decade (e.g., Tiny Tim, Rosemary Clooney). In addition to the "easy–hard" dichotomy, the famous faces test included photographs of some individuals early and late in their careers. For example, photographs of Marlon Brando from the 1950s and 1970s were both included in the test battery.

When this retrograde battery was administered to a group of 11 alcoholic Korsakoff patients and a group of 15 normal control subjects who were matched to the amnesics for age and educational background, little evidence supporting Sanders and Warrington's (1971) contentions was found. As shown in Figures 1.2 and 1.3, the classical gradient was evident, regardless of the difficulty of the items. For both easy and hard items, the alcoholic Korsakoff patients identified more photographs from the 1930s and 1940s than from the 1960s (Figure 1.2). On the recall questionnaire (Figure 1.3), the same gradients emerge.

When Albert *et al.* (1979) assessed the patients' ability to identify photographs of famous people early and late in their careers, further evidence of the sparing of remote memories was found. Although

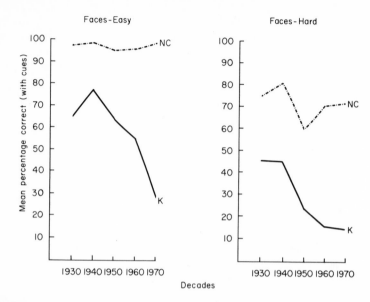

FIGURE 1.2 *The diagrams show the mean percentage of easy and hard items identified correctly by normal controls (NC) and Korsakoff alcoholics (K) using the Famous Faces Test.*

the normal control group was more accurate at identifying famous people late rather than earlier in their careers, the alcoholic Korsakoff patients performed in the opposite manner. The alcoholic Korsakoff patients were more likely to identify Marlon Brando as he appeared in the 1950s rather than as he looked in the late 1960s or early 1970s.

On the basis of the Albert *et al.* (1979) study and the other investigations reviewed, it seems fair to conclude that temporal gradients do exist in the retrograde memory deficits of at least some amnesic patients. Whether the gradients reported for alcoholic Korsakoff patients (Albert *et al.*, 1979; Marslen-Wilson & Teuber, 1975; Seltzer & Benson, 1974) are also characteristic of other groups of amnesic patients (e.g., postencephalitics) remains to be determined and will be a topic of discussion in Chapter 8.

The Korsakoff patients' tendency to *confabulate* when faced with questions they cannot answer is an often-cited characteristic of their disorder. When asked to recall their activities of the previous day, Korsakoff patients may "fill in" this gap in their memory with a story concerning a trip to their home or to a sporting event that may actually have occurred many years ago. This confabulatory tendency

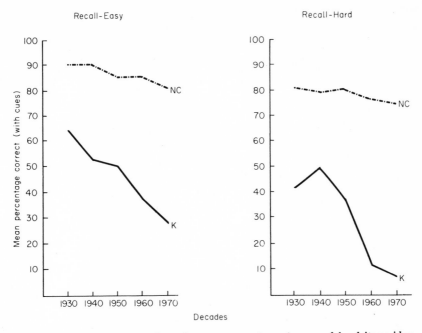

FIGURE 1.3 *The diagrams show the mean percentage of easy and hard items iden-tified correctly by normal controls (NC) and Korsakoff alcoholics (K) using the Recall Questionnaire.*

is not a constant or necessarily permanent feature of amnesic patients, and there are marked individual differences among amnesic popula-tions. In general, confabulation is most marked during the acute stages of the illness and becomes progressively less noticeable as patients adjust to their disorder. It is relatively easy to elicit confabula-tion from a patient in a Wernicke-Korsakoff confusional state, but such responses are rare in chronic alcoholic Korsakoff patients who have had this disease for 5 or more years. Certainly, the notion that confabulation is a cardinal symptom of Korsakoff's syndrome is not consistent with our experience with such patients.

Despite the severity of Korsakoff patients' memory impairments, their intellectual functions, as measured by standardized IQ tests, often remain relatively intact. Therefore, it is important to dis-tinguish at this point the alcoholic Korsakoff patient from the patient with alcoholic dementia. Patients with alcoholic dementia demon-strate a general and severe intellectual decline associated with their decades of alcohol abuse, and their memory problems do not stand

7

TABLE 1.1

Mean Performance of Alcoholic Korsakoff Patients and Nonalcoholics on the WAIS

	Korsakoff	Nonalcoholic controls
Age	53.4	53.2
Years of education	10.77	10.88
Full scale WAIS	102.55	99.22
Verbal IQ	105.33	99.77
Performance IQ	98.55	97.22
Information	10.66	10.55
Comprehension	11.55	9.00
Arithmetic	9.66	9.55
Similarities	10.55	9.44
Digit-span	9.44	8.77
Vocabulary	10.77	9.77
Digit-symbol	3.44	6.88
Picture completion	9.55	9.77
Block design	8.22	7.77
Picture arrangement	7.77	7.77
Object assembly	8.66	6.55

out as the most noticeable and debilitating symptom of their disorder. Table 1.1 shows the performances of nine alcoholic Korsakoff patients and nine intact normal control subjects on the Wechsler Adult Intelligence Scale (WAIS). The two groups have been matched on the basis of age (mean = 53 years), socioeconomic class (working class), and educational background (mean = 11 years of formal education). Except for the digit-symbol subtest, there are no significant differences between the Korsakoffs and the normal controls. Special notice should be made of the Korsakoffs' normal performance on the digit span subtest, a task that is often considered a measure of immediate memory. Drachman and Arbit (1966) have demonstrated that postencephalitic patients, like normal individuals, can repeat 7 or 8 numbers immediately after presentation, but are severely impaired in attempting to learn supraspan lists of 12 numbers. Presumably, once the list has been lengthened to include 12 numbers, the first 3 or 4 numbers can no longer be in working memory, but rather must be retained in a more permanent long-term storage.

Figure 1.4 shows the verbal IQ, performance IQ, full-scale IQ, and memory quotient (MQ based upon the Wechsler Memory Scale) of 9 alcoholic Korsakoff patients, 47 long-term alcoholics (non-Korsakoff),

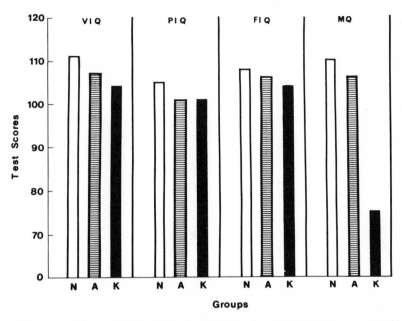

FIGURE 1.4 *The graphs illustrate the WAIS verbal (VIQ), performance (PIQ), and full-scale (FIQ) intelligence scores, and Wechsler Memory Quotients (MQ) of normal controls (N), alcoholics (A), and Korsakoff alcoholics (K).*

and 28 normal individuals. Again, there are no significant differences between the alcoholic Korsakoff patients and the other two groups on the IQ scores, although the MQs of the alcoholic Korsakoff patients are clearly impaired. This 20–30 point scatter between IQ and MQ is the psychometric hallmark of the amnesic symptomatology of alcoholic Korsakoff patients.

Despite their normal IQ, the cognitive performance of the alcoholic Korsakoff patient is not completely intact. A full neuropsychological evaluation usually reveals a number of secondary defects that may or may not contribute to the patients' severe memory problems. The most common deficits involve visuoperceptive and visuospatial capacities. Alcoholic Korsakoff patients are dramatically impaired on digit-symbol and symbol-digit substitution tasks (Glosser, Butters, & Kaplan, 1977; Kapur & Butters, 1977; Talland, 1965), on hidden or embedded figures tests (Glosser *et al.,* 1977; Kapur & Butters, 1977; Talland, 1965), and on various tests requiring the sorting and discrimination of complex visual stimuli (Oscar-Berman, 1973; Oscar-Berman & Samuels, 1977). Such visuoperceptive deficits should not be surprising, as chronic alcoholics who are not clinically amnesic have been reported to have the same perceptual problems (e.g., Goldstein & Shelly, 1971; Goodwin & Hill, 1975; Kleinknecht & Goldstein, 1972; Parsons, 1975; Parsons, Tarter, & Jones, 1971). Although there are some indications that these visuoperceptive deficits, like the patients' memory disorders, may be due to atrophy of limbic structures surrounding the third ventricle (Jarho, 1973), many investigators have attributed these perceptual disorders to atrophy of cortical association areas (e.g., Parsons, 1975; Parsons *et al.*, 1971).

No description of the alcoholic Korsakoffs patients' major psychological symptoms would be complete without some mention of the patients' *personality changes.* These patients often have premorbid histories of psychopathic behavior characterized by impulsive aggressive acts and petty crimes designed to support their chronic alcoholism. Many were "bar room brawlers" who also violently attacked members of their immediate families. With the onset of Korsakoff's syndrome, a dramatic change occurs in these motivational–affective characteristics. Instead of impulsivity, aggression, and severe alcohol abuse, we see apathy, passivity, a lack of initiative, and a virtual disinterest in alcohol. The patient is also unable to formulate or organize a series of plans. Left to his or her own devices, the patient is likely to remain seated before a television set, or even in bed, for long periods of time. They make few demands or inquiries of hospital staff and will obey all instructions in a passive but indifferent manner. This lack of spontaneity and emotional affect make them ideal subjects for neuropsychological studies. Very rarely do alcoholic Korsakoff patients complain of the dullness or seeming irrelevance of the cognitive tasks they are repeatedly asked to complete. The apathy of the Korsakoff patient is not the consequence of institutionalization: Their personality change is apparent shortly after they enter the Korsakoff phase of their illness, and occurs even in patients who return to their home environments.

One of the most perplexing and least investigated questions raised by the study of Korsakoff patients concerns the relationship between their personality changes and their cognitive deficits. Talland (1965) has proposed that the Korsakoff patient's difficulties in memory and perception are due to a faulty organization of cognitive strategies (i.e., a perseveration or rigidity of cognitive sets) resulting from a premature closure of activating mechanisms. That is, the patients' motivational and arousal deficits prevent a thorough coding of new information (anterograde amnesia) and the organization of suitable search strategies for scanning stored information (retrograde amnesia). Because it is commonly believed that arousal and attentional processes are dependent upon the reticular activating system (RAS), Talland assumed that the Korsakoff patient's midline diencephalic lesions interrupted the RAS's positive influence on cognitive (i.e., cortical) functions.

Granted that attentional factors may be responsible for some of the Korsakoff patients' cognitive problems, it remains unlikely that most of their amnesia can be explained by such concepts. Patients with frontal lobe lesions, including those who have undergone frontal lobotomies, also develop personality characteristics similar to those of the Korsakoff patients, yet fail to evidence the striking amnesic symptoms. If impairments in activation can occur without a concomitant change in memory functions, some skepticism must remain regarding the extent to which the Korsakoff patients' personality change influences their cognitive performance.

NEUROPATHOLOGY

There have been several reviews of the neuropathology of the Wernicke-Korsakoff syndrome (Brierley, 1977; Victor, Adams, & Collins, 1971), and we shall only outline their major findings and conclusions. As Brierley (1977) notes, most of the literature supports the conclusion that the neurological symptoms of Wernicke's encephalopathy are related to lesions of the brain stem and cerebellum, whereas the amnesic symptoms of the chronic Korsakoff state involve damage to several thalamic and hypothalamic structures surrounding the third ventricle of the brain. The dorsomedial nucleus of the thalamus and the mammillary bodies of the hypothalamus are the specific structures most often associated with the alcoholic Korsakoff patient's amnesic symptoms. Figure 1.5 is an outline drawing of two coronal brain sections in which the third ventricle, the dorsomedial nucleus of the thalamus, and the mammillary bodies are clearly labeled.

Gamper (1928) studied the brains of 16 alcoholic Korsakoff patients and found that their lesions extended from the thalamus to the

11

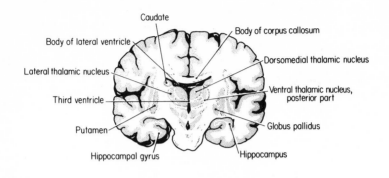

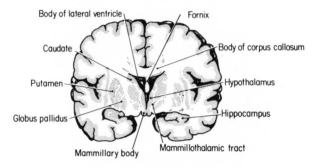

FIGURE 1.5 *The illustrations are of coronal sections through the human brain. The* dorsomedial nucleus of the thalamus *(top section) and the* mammillary bodies *(bottom section) are the two structures most frequently associated with the amnesic symptoms of Korsakoff's syndrome.*

lower brainstem. He noted much variation from case to case, but concluded that the mammillary bodies were the crucial structure as all 16 Korsakoff patients had extensive atrophy of these nuclei. No correlations between brain pathology and clinical symptoms were reported.

Riggs and Boles (1944) examined 29 brains of patients who had "Wernicke's disease." Although alcohol abuse was associated with nearly half these cases, the remaining cases were due to a number of other causes (e.g., prolonged vomiting). The neuropathological findings showed that the mammillary bodies were affected in 21 of 23 cases, the dorsomedial nucleus of the thalamus in 23 of 27, and the pulvinar of the thalamus in 10 of 14.

Delay, Brion, and Elissalde (1958 a, b) described the neuropathology of eight alcoholic Korsakoff patients with both anterograde and retrograde memory deficits. Atrophy of the mammillary bodies was common to all cases, but significant thalamic involvement was noted in only one brain. These investigators stressed the lack of consistent cortical pathology, and pointed to the mammillary bodies as the most probable source of the patients' amnesic symptoms.

Adams, Collins, and Victor (1962) combined neuropathological findings with careful clinical and psychometric examinations of 300 Wernicke-Korsakoff patients. They found that the onset of the Wernicke stage was acute and subsided rapidly with the administration of large doses of thiamine. As the confusion, ataxia, nystagmus, and ocular palsies cleared, the patients' major remaining symptoms were severe anterograde and retrograde amnesias. Of the 300 cases, 54 brains were eventually studied. The investigators attributed the symptoms of Wernicke's disease to lesions in the brainstem (e.g., oculomotor nucleus) and cerebellum. The severe memory disorder of the Korsakoff stage was correlated with the presence of lesions in the mammillary bodies and several thalamic nuclei (e.g., dorsomedial, anteroventral, and pulvinar).

In another report, Victor, Adams, and Collins (1971) examined the brains of 82 Wernicke-Korsakoff patients who had been carefully studied in terms of clinical symptomatology. Central to our interest in the neuroanatomical basis of the patients' amnesia were the results for the dorsomedial nucleus of the thalamus, which was examined in 43 of these brains. In 38 of the 43 brains, extensive atrophy of the dorsomedial nucleus was noted, but in the 5 brains without atrophy there was no lasting memory disorder. As all 5 of these "negative" cases (as well as the 38 remaining cases) showed severe atrophy of the mammillary bodies, Victor et al. (1971) concluded that the dorsomedial nucleus, and not the mammillary bodies, is the critical structure for the amnesic symptomatology. It should be noted, however, that another interpretation can be drawn from the presented data. Because all 38 cases with amnesia had lesions in both the mammillary bodies and the dorsomedial nucleus of the thalamus, it is possible that this combined thalamic–hypothalamic lesion is the one that is both necessary and sufficient to produce Korsakoff's amnesia. To demonstrate the primacy of the dorsomedial nucleus, it would be necessary to have amnesic cases with atrophy limited to the dorsomedial nucleus. Victor et al. do not report any cases meeting this criterion.

ETIOLOGY

Despite the evidence that Wernicke-Korsakoff's syndrome is related to specific subcortical lesions, the etiology of this brain damage remains obscure. Victor, Adams, and their colleagues (for reviews, Brierley, 1977; Dreyfus, 1974; Victor *et al.*, 1971) have gathered considerable data that points to a thiamine (vitamin B_1) deficiency as the primary factor in this disease. As chronic alcoholics often fail to eat nutritionally balanced diets, malnutrition and avitaminosis are common correlates of chronic alcohol abuse. According to this nutritional theory, the diencephalon, the brainstem, and the cerebellum are very sensitive to thiamine deficiencies and either atrophy or become prone to hemorrhagic lesions.

There are three principle forms of evidence to support this theory of avitaminosis. One, the symptoms of the Wernicke's stage occur commonly in disorders that interfere with food metabolism and absorption. Protracted vomiting during pregnancy, carcinoma of the stomach, chronic gastritis, and intestinal obstruction are some of the disorders associated both with malnutrition and the previously described Wernicke's symptoms.

Two, treatment of Wernicke-Korsakoff patients with large amounts of thiamine alleviates some of the patients' symptoms. Opthalmoplegia and the confusional state begin to improve within a few hours after the administration of thiamine and usually clear within 7 days. The patients' nystagmus and ataxia show a slower and more limited improvement, and these symptoms may still be apparent in a mild form months or even years after the beginning of treatment. Of the various symptoms comprising the Wernicke-Korsakoff syndrome, the memory and personality changes remain the most resistant to thiamine therapy. Eighty percent of all Korsakoff patients show little, if any, improvement in their memory disorder and general apathy despite prolonged administration of vitamins. In fact, the amnesic disorder remains the chronic lifelong disability of the alcoholic Korsakoff patient. Victor *et al.* (1971) believe that this marked variability in the reversibility of symptoms with vitamin therapy reflects differences in the stages of pathology. They conclude that symptoms associated with the Wernicke stage are reversible because they are due to a "biochemical abnormality that has stopped short of significant structural change," whereas the memory disorders of the Korsakoff stage of the illness are irreversi-

dure, 3–12 letters are presented tachistoscopically for very brief periods of time (50–500 msec). Following presentation, subjects are asked to report as many of the digits as they can possibly recall. Sperling found that the average maximum number of digits that a subject could report was 4.3, regardless of the number of digits in the array. At this time, Sperling questioned whether this finding was due to a perceptual limitation or to the capacity of sensory memory. His conclusion that it was probably the latter was based on evidence from a partial recall procedure he developed. Sperling's partial recall procedure involved a partial report technique in which subjects were required to report back the digits from one of three rows viewed. Subjects are cued as to which row they must report only after the display has disappeared. Sperling reasoned that if the subjects had perceptual limitations then recall would be all or none, depending on the row they focused on during presentation and the row they were asked to recall. However, if memory load capacity was the minimizing factor, then the subjects should be able to recall most of any row because the memory capacity would never be exceeded. The results showed that subjects could correctly identify 3–4 items from any row if cued immediately after presentation. As we shall see in the next section of this chapter, this ability disappeared rapidly as the interval between presentation and report was increased. However, the fact that recall for any row was present immediately after the display ended favored the memory capacity limitation theory.

The capacity of STM was most elegantly studied by Miller in 1956. Miller felt that seven items is the upper limit on the amount of material an individual can retain in an unanalyzed, uncategorized state. For example, he found that most people can remember approximately seven random numbers after they are presented at a continuous and rather rapid rate (this of course is often called one's "digit span"). This upper limit seems to hold for randomly presented words, letters, and many other kinds of stimuli. Actually, Miller found the "magic" number seven was not absolute, but that the limit depended on the nature of the material to be remembered and upon the individual. Therefore, he defined the limit of STM as an interval of seven plus or minus two items.

In this important article, Miller also described an experiment in which subjects watched a series of lights go on and off in a random sequence. As expected, he found that the subjects could remember the sequence up to about seven lights, but that they broke down beyond that point. However, he then found that a group of computer technicians were able to reproduce a series of 21 (or even more) such "light-flash" events. They were able to do this by using a binary code to retain one number for a set of 3 lights. Thus, the sequence of 21 lights was really comprised of "seven" numbers, each representing three events. Miller concluded that our short-term capacity can be extended by chunking material into what he called information-rich "bits." We are still limited by the number of bits we can hold, but each bit can contain more than just a single item.

Long-term capacity has generally been described as being infinite, or at least unmeasurable. This has not been meant to imply that everything, once learned, is somewhere in memory. Rather, it means that the amount that can be placed in long-term memory never reaches a fixed limit. At one time, there was a rather folksy belief in circulation that at some point in life each new fact replaced (by bumping out) an old fact, but this belief has been largely discredited by research in memory since the time of Ebbinghaus. Most psychologists and educators now realize that the more we know, the easier it becomes to learn and remember new facts because we have something to relate them to and to aid in their organization. Thus, the capacity of long-term memory seems to be expanding at all times and, consequently, remains infinite.

Information Loss

Theories of memory not only had to stipulate the capacity of each memory system, but also had to explain the mechanism, or mechanisms, responsible for the loss of information from each system when the system's capacity was not overloaded. In other words, the question to be asked was, why an individual would forget information that at one time resided in sensory, short- or long-term memory when the appropriate systems' capacity was not overloaded? To explain this loss, two mechanisms were proposed and, for some time, existed in the literature side by side. Each was originally proposed as the mechanism underlying information loss from LTM, but in time, each came to be invoked as a possible explanation for loss from other memory systems as well. The first theory was called *decay* theory, because it stated that forgetting was simply a fading of an item's representation over time. The other theory was called *interference* theory, because it proposed, originally, that a competition among stored items in memory caused forgetting.

Most evidence derived from LTM favored interference as the primary mechanism producing the loss of information from that system, but decay also had its proponents. In STM, interference and decay have both been demonstrated; although again, each theory has supporters voicing claims that one process alone produces forgetting. The favored theory, however, is one suggesting that forgetting from STM is an "interaction" of interference and decay. Information loss from sensory memory appears to be primarily attributable to decay, with the rate of decay being extremely rapid as demonstrated using the Sperling (1960) paradigm. Thus, at one end of the spectrum (LTM) interference is felt to be the dominant factor; at the other end (sensory memory), decay is the most prevalent explanation; and in between (STM), an interaction is postulated. In order to see how these theories developed, one must look first at studies of LTM in which the mechanisms were first defined and were most extensively investigated.

Prior to significant research on memory, the prevalent opinion was that material forgotten from LTM simply faded away. This theory was also held by Thorndike (1913), who postulated a Law of Disuse to explain forgetting that paralleled his Law of Effect (used to explain acquisition). Thorndike believed that the bond learned between a stimulus and its response weakened over time simply through disuse. Today, this theory would be called the decay theory, and, although it can still claim several proponents, it has not been widely accepted as an explanation of long-term forgetting. Although it is true that retention becomes progressively worse over time, behavioral scientists have been loathe to accept the notion that time, itself, causes this disintegration.

In 1932, McGeoch proposed that competition produced by the learning of new material during a retention interval causes forgetting from LTM. In other words, McGeoch felt that once something is learned it is never forgotten, but other similar learning can compete with this material at recall, and in effect, block a person's ability to retrieve it. Today this condition would be termed "interference," but the underlying rationale of competition still remains.

Interference was felt to be due solely to competition until the forties, when Melton and Irwin (1940) questioned whether the effects of retroactive interference (RI) could indeed be due only to this one variable. They had no argument with the attribution of the effects of proactive interference (PI) to competition, as the interfering material in that case is learned prior to the to-be-remembered (TBR) material. However, in RI, the interfering material is actually learned after the TBR material, and Melton and Irwin felt that perhaps the learning of the interfering task might, in and of itself, have an effect on the retention of the TBR material. Subjects might actually be forced to "unlearn" some of the earlier learned material while they are learning the new task. Therefore, when subjects are asked to recall the older material they find that because of this unlearning, they are unable to retrieve it.

Melton and Irwin tested their assumption by varying the number of trials given on an interpolated task in an RI paradigm. Their subjects learned a serial list of consonant–vowel–consonant trigrams (CVCs), and then, after 0–50 trials on a second list, they were asked for recall of the first list of CVCs. The number of interpolated task intrusions during the recall of Task A was recorded as well as the total number of errors. Melton and Irwin discovered that the number of overt competition responses (the intrusions) increased at first but then dropped off to nearly zero. Therefore, they proposed that something else must be responsible for the increasing amount of RI. Melton and Irwin mysteriously labeled this additional variable Factor X, but researchers quickly began to attribute the additional increase in RI to the phenomena of unlearning (Barnes & Underwood, 1959; Briggs, 1954).

It can be seen that by the late 1950s interference had not only become the pervading theory of retention loss from long-term memory, but the factors which contributed to two types of interference (RI and PI) had also been well defined. Researchers had begun their attempts to explain forgetting from STM and, as they had in theories of LTM, the "early" investigators seemed to favor a decay interpretation. One of the first systematic attempts to explore the factors which contribute to short-term forgetting was made by Peterson and Peterson in 1959. Their procedure (which came to be called the distractor technique and is discussed later in this chapter) began by briefly presenting verbal material, for example, a consonant trigram (CCC), to their subjects. This presentation was followed immediately by a second task that was designed to prevent rehearsal of the TBR material. After 3–18 sec of this distracting activity, the subject was asked to try to recall the stimulus item. In this way, the course of forgetting the CCC could be tracked by testing its retention at various time intervals. Peterson and Peterson found that the probability of correct recall decreased as the length of the retention interval increased (Figure 2.1). This led them to their conclusion that decay was the principle cause of forgetting in STM.

The error of their assumption was quickly pointed out by Keppel

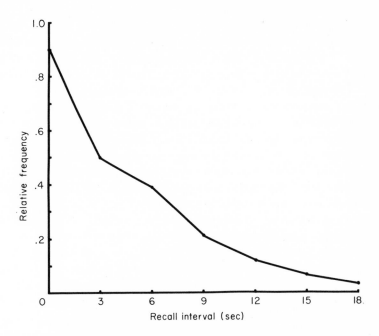

FIGURE 2.1 *The graph illustrates the frequency of correct recalls of consonant trigrams CCCs with latencies below 2.83 sec as a function of the recall interval.*

and Underwood (1962), who showed that the Petersons had over-looked an important source of "interference" in their design, namely, the PI that accrued from items presented on preceding trials. Keppel and Underwood argued that because the Petersons had given their subjects several practice trials before initiating their testing procedure, a good deal of PI had been generated prior to the point at which they began to collect data. Therefore, Keppel and Underwood developed a procedure that eliminated these practice effects and demonstrated the role of interference in determining the rate of forgetting in STM.

Keppel and Underwood tested their subjects for only six trials with no practice trials allowed. They tested one group following a 3-sec interval and one group after an 18-sec interval. They discovered that, at least for the 18-sec group, a gradual build-up of interference accrued across the six trials (as indicated by the fact that retention dropped from nearly 100% of Trial 1 to approximately 40% on Trial 6). If decay were the only variable determining the forgetting rate, then the amount forgotten should have been the same on Trial 1 as

23

on the final trial. Instead, Keppel and Underwood found that as the number of preceding trials increased, the amount retained decreased. This, coupled with their report that the majority of intrusions came from previously presented items, led them to propose that STM follows the same laws of interference as does LTM.

At about the same time, Murdock (1961) pointed out a second way in which the effects of interference could be demonstrated using the distractor technique. Rather than varying the number of prior trials as Keppel and Underwood had done, he varied the amount of information the subject had to retain on any one trial. Murdock reasoned that if decay were the only factor causing forgetting in STM, then the rate of retention loss for one word should be the same as that for three words. However, he discovered that this simply was not the case. In fact, one word was rarely lost over an 18-sec retention interval (regardless of number of prior trials), whereas the retention of three words displayed the same dramatic curve as the retention of CCCs had for the Petersons.

The only question left unanswered by Murdock's research was why the effects of interference become more prevalent as the length of the retention interval increased. One possible explanation for this effect came from an analogy provided by Posner (1967), who likened the distractor situation to an acid bath. He pointed out that it is well known that the rate at which metal dissolves in acid is a function of the strength of the acid. He proposed that, similarly, the amount of forgetting in the STM distractor technique may be a joint function of the strength of the interference (acid) that is present during the time new information is introduced, and the length of time that elapses between presentation and recall. Thus, forgetting in STM would truly be an interaction between decay and interference.

Once it had been shown that interference exists in both STM and LTM, it became important for investigators to attempt to determine whether the interference that was effective in producing forgetting in LTM was the same as that for STM. Melton (1963) was among the first to argue that the effects were the same as type and amount of interference appeared to determine the amount forgotten in both LTM and STM. However, Conrad (1962) argued that, although LTM was known to be susceptible primarily to semantic effects, the interference effective in STM was largely of an acoustic nature. Conrad demonstrated the effects of acoustic interference in STM by presenting six letters to his subjects, and then having them attempt to recall the letters in the order of presentation. He found that, for the most part, the subjects' errors tended to "sound like" the correct responses. In other words, a p was more likely to be recalled in place of a b than was an h. Wickelgren (1965) extended this same analysis to include numbers and again found interference to be of an acoustic nature. These results led Baddeley and Dale (1966) and Adams (1967) to conclude that interference in STM is different from that in LTM, in that it is based upon acoustic as opposed to semantic relationships.

In order to study the rate of information loss in sensory memory, Sperling (1960) modified his technique and delayed the point at which the subject was cued to recall the display, or portion of the display. As explained earlier, Sperling had demonstrated that a subject could recall only 4.3 items of information (usually letters) from a 3 × 4 array. By cueing for particular rows, he showed that more information was available than could actually be recited. From this, he had reasoned that perhaps the information in the array was lost after the subject was able to recite 4–5 letters. However, he could not ascertain whether this was due to the "interference" produced by recalling letters, or by the "time" it took to get them out. In order to explore these possibilities, Sperling developed the partial report technique coupled with a delay of cue.

In his new procedure, Sperling delayed the cue either 0, .15, .30, or 1.0 sec after stimulus offset. The subject had to try to retain as much of the display as possible because he did not know which row he would have to recall. The results of this procedure can be seen in Figure 2.2. After 1 sec, the subject could retrieve only about 1.4 items per row. If this is multiplied by the number of rows in the display, the amount of information left to the subject can be calculated. Interestingly enough the 4.2 items left to him is approximately the same amount he was able to recall when using the complete report. This means that his processing limitation is a function, not of perception, but of the rate at which items decay from sensory memory. Apparently, in the complete recall condition the subject remembers only 4.3 items because after that the rest of the information that was initially available has decayed. This effect occurs even on the first trial of the task, and (as the subject does not engage in a distractor task during the 1-sec retention interval) it must be that a true decay effect has been demonstrated.

By using a somewhat modified version of this partial report procedure, Averbach and Coriell (1961) and Averbach and Sperling (1961)

25

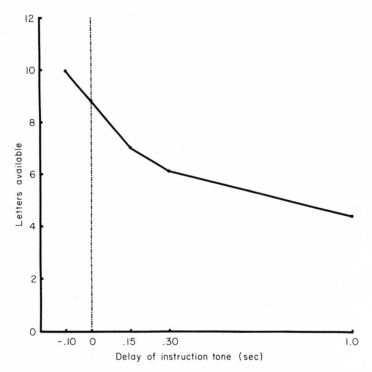

FIGURE 2.2 *The graph illustrates the decay of available information (items re-called) using partial report as a function of the delay of the recall cue (tone).*

have shown that the trace (or *icon*) produced during the brief presentation interval not only decays rapidly, but can be interfered with as well. In the Averbach and Coriell experiment, two rows of eight letters each were presented to the subject for 50 msec. A circle appeared 50–200 msec later and the subject's task was to name the letter that had appeared within the area outlined by the circle.

The subjects in this experiment reported that when the circle appeared surrounding the position of the letter, the trace of the item seemed to be "wiped out." This effect occurred most dramatically when the circle appeared 100–200 msec after the letter. If it appeared prior to this time, the subject reported that the two images seemed to be superimposed on one another so that both were seen together. When the circle appeared more than 200 msec after the letter, the trace of the letter was already processed beyond the iconic stage, and so it did not have the same appearance of having been wiped out. It was only in the short 100–200 msec range that the image of the circle seemed to erase the not fully processed trace of the letter. This result led Averbach and Sperling (1961) to conclude that the life span of an icon is approximately 250 msec. Beyond this time, a more permanent memory trace must begin to be formed, as the subject perhaps begins to rehearse whatever it is that he has read out from his iconic storage.

Physiological Evidence

Physiological evidence for the separation of memory stores has largely centered upon the distinction between STM and LTM, with little or no research being performed on sensory memory. Evidence from studies of amnesic patients has often been cited as being the most substantial support for the classical distinction between LTM and STM (Cermak, 1972; Wickelgren, 1973). Milner (1959) was among the first to demonstrate that when the hippocampus is damaged or destroyed bilaterally, the patient becomes unable to learn or remember any new information. Such patients can still retain some information through constant rehearsal, as long as they are not distracted, and provided the task does not exceed their item span. The patients' STM capacity remains nearly normal, but their LTM capacity seems to be completely depleted. Thus, these patients can "retain" only a small amount of continually rehearsed material and are not able to chunk it into bits, nor can they transfer it into a more permanent storehouse (LTM). This existence of an intact processing system (STM) in the presence of a totally deficient storage system (LTM) has been used as evidence that STM and LTM must represent two independent storage systems.

Further support for this distinction comes from the research of Warrington and Shallice (1969), who reported the interesting case of a patient (K.F.) who had suffered damage to his left parietal-occipital region. This patient displayed a decreased digit span (three items) but retained a fairly decent LTM ability. He could learn new information and his free recall was very nearly normal. This case then, which is an example of normal LTM in the presence of limited STM, provides converse physiological evidence for the two-component view of memory.

It must be emphasized again, however, that the physiological evidence presented here supports only the "capacity" differential. It does not speak to the purported difference in susceptibility to the effects of decay and interference between the two systems. This latter issue will be discussed in some detail in the next two chapters.

SHORT-TERM–LONG-TERM-MEMORY PARADIGMS FREQUENTLY USED IN AMNESIA RESEARCH

Some verbal-memory paradigms have been used so frequently by investigators of amnesic symptomatology that they deserve special attention before the results emanating from their application can be discussed. Consequently, before turning to a further description of the research performed on amnesics' LTM, some of these paradigms used to study both LTM and STM will be outlined. Because few studies have been performed on amnesics' sensory memory, the specialized paradigms used in those studies will be left for later description.

Long-Term-Memory Paradigms

Three techniques have been used more frequently than any others as methods for presenting verbal material to patients. The first, called the paired-associate (P-A) technique, is similar in procedure to the manner in which flash cards are used as aids in learning a foreign vocabulary. The second technique is serial presentation, a procedure similar to the one followed in learning the order of the presidents of the United States, in that it involves having to learn what follows what in a list of words. The final method, free learning, is similar to the party game in which many items are displayed on a tray for several seconds and then the guests must record, in any order, as many items as possible.

PAIRED-ASSOCIATES

In paired-associate (P-A) learning, each stimulus and its corresponding response are presented on a memory drum apparatus or by means of a slide projector. The patient is shown a word, a number, a consonant followed by a vowel and another consonant (CVC), or a consonant trigram (CCC) for a few seconds. This material is immediately followed by the presentation (also for several seconds) of the same stimulus paired with a response. The response could be any type of verbal material, of the same type as the stimulus or different. Other P-A's are then presented following the same procedure: first stimulus alone, then stimulus plus response. After the last items are presented, the list starts over and a new trial begins. On this second trial, the patient is asked to anticipate which response will be paired with each stimulus. He does this when the stimulus is presented alone, and, as the items are not presented in the same order from trial to trial, he is told to learn the pairings and not the order of presentation. The patient generally continues to be shown the list until he can correctly anticipate each response on one trial (or, sometimes, on two consecutive trials). The measures of learning that are usually computed are the number of trials to criterion, or the number of correct responses at the end of a fixed number of trials.

The method just described as the usual method for presenting P-A's is called the *anticipation method*. An alternative P-A procedure is to present each pair, one at a time for perhaps 4 sec, and then to show only the stimulus member of each pair. At the end of the trial the patient is asked to supply the response to each of the stimuli. This method, called the *study-test method,* also presents the pairs in different orders from trial to trial, but tests at the conclusion of each presentation trial rather than during the trial itself.

SERIAL LEARNING

Serial learning differs from P-A learning in one important way, that is, the order of presentation must be learned rather than associative units. In serial learning, the patient is asked to observe a list of materials (e.g., 12 words) and to note not only what material is presented but also the order in which it is presented. Following the initial presentation trial, the patient is told that his task will be to try to anticipate each item in the list just prior to its presentation. Trials continue until the patient can correctly anticipate each item on two consecutive trials. Again, as with P-A learning, the measures that are usually taken are the numbers of trials to criterion, or the number of correct responses after a fixed number of trials.

The study–test method is also used to assess serial learning. This technique (Runquist, 1966) presents the material in a serial order, but instructs the patient to recall the items, in order, at the conclusion of each trial, rather than during presentation. Trials continue until the patient learns all the material or until a specified number of trials have been concluded.

FREE LEARNING

Unlike the preceding forms of stimulus presentation, free learning does not ask patients to associate materials, nor do they have to learn the order of the material. Instead, the subject is shown the stimuli one at a time, or is given a certain period of time (e.g., 2 min for 20 words) to inspect all the material. Then, at the end of the presentation period, the subject is asked to recall as many of the items as he can, in any order. The measures employed with the preceding methods of presentation are used here as well.

Measures of Retention in Long-Term Memory

Amnesic patients' retention has been tested using several different methods, the most commonly used being recall, recognition, and relearning. All three of these dependent variables are used to estimate the amount of information retained following a specified retention interval. There is a controversy as to whether these three measures are actually three different ways of tapping the same memory reserve, or whether they constitute three taps of three separate reserves, but that issue will be set aside at this time.

RECALL

There are two types of recall: free recall (FR) and cued recall (CR). In *free recall,* patients are asked to produce as much as they possibly can of the material they were asked to learn, without being given prompts or cues. For instance, patients might be asked to recite a list of words they had learned a few minutes previously. In *cued recall,* the patient is helped in some way to recall the material. For example, several hours after learning a 12-item P-A task, patients may be tested by being provided with cues for the responses not unavailable through FR. These cues take many forms, such as the rhyme of a correct response or a word from the same category. This is still considered to be a recall task because, although the patient's retrieval of the response is aided, the actual response is not given.

RECOGNITION

A recognition test differs from a recall test in that it provides the correct response embedded within a list of several other alternatives. The patient must choose the correct response from among these alternatives during a specified retrieval period. In other words, instead of having to try to recall the responses on his own, the patient is provided a set of responses from which to choose. The task could be either:

to select which responses he learned, or to tell which responses were originally paired with which stimuli, or to arrange the responses in a particular order. In any case, retention is measured on the basis of the number of responses recognized correctly, minus a correction for guessing based on the number of alternatives provided.

RELEARNING

The relearning method, frequently called the savings method, is based on the assumption that if a patient can relearn material at a rate faster than he had originally learned it, then some material must have been retained from the original learning session. The amount that is retained, or saved, is expressed by the formula:

$$\text{Savings Score} = 100 \times \frac{\text{Original trials} - \text{Relearning trials}}{\text{Original trials}}$$

As can be seen, when no relearning trials are necessary, the savings score is 100%. When it takes as much time to relearn as it took to learn, retention is scored at 0%.

Short-Term-Memory Paradigms

As discussed previously, the most popular presentation technique used for studying STM (or at least for studying the rate of forgetting from STM) has been the distractor technique developed by Peterson and Peterson (1959). In this procedure, information in an amount well below the patient's STM capacity (usually three letters, three words, or even a single word) is presented briefly to the patient, usually for about 2 sec. This is immediately followed by a task designed to prevent the patient from rehearsing the TBR material. This "distracting" task often consists of counting backward from a predetermined number such as 100 by ones or threes; the patient may also be asked to name colors from a color chart, or listen to a taped reading of letters, numbers or words, in order to detect when a particular stimulus occurs. This rehearsal-preventing task generally lasts between 3 and 20 sec and then the patient is asked to try to recall the TBR items. As in the case of LTM paradigms, FR or CR can be used and, in some cases, a recognition task is given.

Occasionally, a serial learning paradigm has also been used to study the STM of amnesics. The relationship between the recall of the final few items of a serially presented list and the recall from the remainder of the list is the factor that has been used to study STM. Murdock (1962) has reported that, for normal subjects, recall of items from the last seven positions of a list is better than that from any other portion of the list except the initial two or three items. This is true regardless of the length of the list or the rate at which the words are presented. Furthermore, Murdock found that the probability of recall of the seven most recently presented items (presumably still in STM) was a decreasing function of the amount of material intervening between presentation of the last TBR item and the time when recall was required. Glanzer and Cunitz (1966) introduced an interesting modification of Murdock's procedure by varying the length of time between the presentation of the last item of a 15-word list and the recall task. They found that the STM component of the FR serial curve was drastically reduced simply by inserting a delay of 10 sec between the end of the list and the signal to recall. If the delay was 30 sec, the whole effect was completely erased. This result is consistent with the acid-bath theory of STM, which stated that the effects of interference in STM increase with time. In addition, it suggests that items in LTM may also be providing interference with the recall of the most recently presented items supposedly in STM. At any rate, the advantage these items gained by their recency are eliminated over time. The paradigm has been used on occasion as a means of studying amnesics' STM by documenting their retrieval of the last several items of a serially presented list.

Other STM techniques, such as Waugh and Norman's (1965) probe-digit procedure and Conrad's (1962) acoustic-confusion matrix paradigm have for one reason or another not been adopted for use with Korsakoff patients. Nor, as has been stated, have many of the sensory memory paradigms. A few paradigms have been developed specifically to study amnesia, but these will be more fully explained, whenever appropriate, in the forthcoming chapters as will the several paradigms developed to study specific features of the amnesics' memory difficulties. The first of these areas of investigation will be the Korsakoff patients' LTM disorder, to which we shall now turn.

3

Long-Term Memory

In Chapter 1, the extent of the alcoholic Korsakoff patient's retrograde amnesia was described. This research documented, among other things, an almost total inability to recall events from the most recent decade preceding testing. It appeared as if little, if anything, had achieved permanent status in the memory repertoire of these patients since the time that their brain damage had been diagnosed as having occurred. Consequently, it would appear that long-term memory research might prove fruitless with these patients because experiment after experiment would show that no information was being retained by these patients. Such an endeavor would be frightfully boring to the research investigator, and even more so to the readers of journals into which such nondocumentation of retention found its way. Therefore, research of this type has not tended to proliferate in the field. What does exist, though, are several reports of instances in which, under the proper conditions, a limited amount of long-term retention can be demonstrated. This retention is not always evident in the free recall of the patients, but it can occasionally be shown to be present under cueing or recognition conditions. As long-term retention is most apparent in paired-associate learning and somewhat less so with serial learning, paired-associate learning will be discussed first.

PAIRED-ASSOCIATE LEARNING

Paired-associate (P-A) learning is routinely administered to all amnesic patients as part of the Wechsler Memory Scale, and it is well known that alcoholic Korsakoff patients perform abysmally on the hard items, but do learn a few of the easier items. However, because the easier items are so predictable, and of such high frequency (e.g., north–south, up–down), it is questionable whether new learning is necessarily tested by this task. The Wechsler test mercifully ends after only three trials because most investigators have discovered that once alcoholic Korsakoff patients begin to perseverate an incorrect response on the less predictable items, they will continue to do so ad infinitum. Not all items are incorrectly perseverated, however, and when a correct item does attain long-term status, it seems to be retained. To further demonstrate this fact, Cermak, Butters and Goodglass (1971) taught their Korsakoff patients a six item P-A list.

In their task, each patient was asked to learn P-A's in which the members of each pair were unrelated monosyllabic words. A maximum of 16 trials was given to each patient, but testing ended if a patient successfully produced a correct response for each stimulus on 2 consecutive trials. This was accomplished for all the control patients but not for any of the Korsakoff patients. Each Korsakoff patient did learn 2 or 3 of the pairs on the task and, more importantly, was able to retain these few items. In fact, those items learned were relearned almost immediately on reintroduction of the test procedure on each of three successive days (see Figure 3.1). In other words, information that achieved long-term memory (LTM) status apparently left enough of a trace so that relearning progressed more rapidly than original learning. This allowed the patients the freedom to pick up more of the P-A's on subsequent days and, interestingly enough, those new items also were relearned quickly the succeeding day. Complete free recall was never possible, but enough of the P-A was retained to accelerate the relearning process.

The Cermak *et al.* (1971) results were consistent with those reported previously by Warrington and Weiskrantz. They found that patients could reidentify partially formed pictures (Warrington & Weiskrantz, 1968b) or words (Weiskrantz & Warrington, 1970a) on the basis of less information during the second administration of the test. In their task, each patient was shown partially formed (incomplete) pictures or words and was asked to identify the stimulus on the basis of this partial information. When the patient failed to do so, a more complete form was presented. This step-wise presentation continued until the patient identified the stimulus. Twenty-four hours later the same procedure was administered. This time, however, patients were consistently able to identify the stimulus sooner than they had the first time the test was given (Figure 3.2). This seemed to indicate that at least some

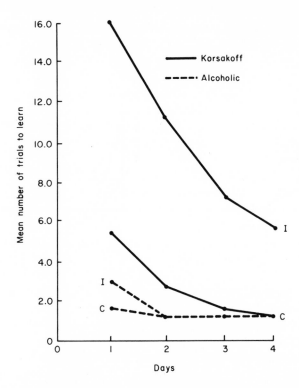

FIGURE 3.1 *The graph illustrates the mean number of trials required to learn particular items on successive days, and contrasts those items learned correctly (C) by alcoholic Korsakoff patients on Day 1 with those that remained incorrect (I). The same matched items are plotted for the alcoholic controls.*

portion of their initial learning experience had been retained, presumably in LTM because at least 1 day had passed since original learning.

Warrington and Weiskrantz (1976) also demonstrated this phenomenon using a task in which the first few letters of a word were used to prompt retrieval of the whole word. This modified P-A task produced exactly the same results as the previous task. However, it must be realized when considering the results of this task, and of all similar tasks, that the amnesics' learning and relearning always lagged considerably behind the normals' and, if tested several months later (as, informally, were Cermak's patients), their performance returned to the level of original learning. It appears, then, that eventually all vestiges of any traces are lost. Precisely how quickly this loss occurs

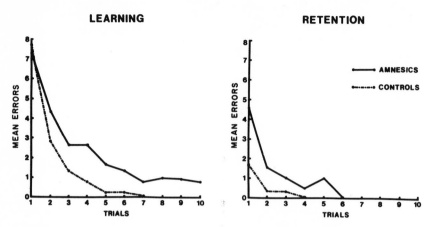

FIGURE 3.2 *The graphs illustrate learning and 24-hour relearning (retention) scores for amnesic and control groups.*

has never been studied, but probably within a matter of days, at least for verbal material.

Recently, Cermak (1975) has compared three different methods of P-A presentation in an attempt to determine whether two variables shown to aid normals' acquisition rate and retentive ability might also facilitate the Korsakoff patients' otherwise ponderous acquisition rate and very poor recall. In this experiment, each Korsakoff patient and a matched alcoholic control (a long-term alcoholic) were instructed to learn to anticipate the correct response to each of five stimuli in a P-A list using one of the following three methods: rote learning, imagery learning, and cued learning. In rote learning the patient simply learned to anticipate the response to each stimulus. In imagery learning, the patient was taught how to form a visual image linking each stimulus and response, and then was told to try to use the image when attempting to recall the response. For example, the patient was asked to imagine an arrow stuck in a tree in order to remember the pair arrow–tree. The patient was reinstructed if he made an error on a given trial. In cued learning, the patient was supplied with a mediating verbal link to the correct response at the time he was shown the stimulus-response pairing, and also at the time of retrieval. For example, he was given the word *wood* as a link between *arrow* and *tree*.

The results indicate that although the alcoholic Korsakoff patients performed more poorly than the controls on all aspects of this test,

TABLE 3.1
*Number of Trials to Criterion for Each Learning Method
and Each Response Measure*

	Learning method	Response measure		
		Number of trials to learn (free recall)	Number of trials to relearn (free recall)	Number of trials to learn (recognition)
Korsakoff patients	Rote	22.5	16.0	9.8
	Imagery	13.5	8.2	3.3
	Cued	13.2	8.5	9.5
Alcoholic controls	Rote	4.7	1.3	1.7
	Imagery	1.3	1.2	1.0
	Cued	2.3	1.3	1.0

some interesting effects did emerge as a function of the type of learning procedure. Table 3.1 shows the number of trials it took to learn under all three conditions, as well as indicating performance on a recognition and a relearning task. The alcoholic Korsakoff patients (as well as the control subjects) performed significantly better using imagery versus rote learning on both the free recall task and a recognition task. They also performed better using mediation on a free recall task, but this technique did not improve performance on a recognition task. Thus, imagery consistently improved both learning and retention, but mediation did so only for the free recall conditions.

From these results, it can be concluded that imagery may be a useful device for facilitating amnesic patients' storage and retrieval of verbal information. The patients can apparently translate the verbal information into a nonverbal image and can then retranslate it into its verbal representation during recall. Baddeley and Warrington (1973) discovered that there is a limit to which amnesics can utilize imagery when they found that their patients could not image four words at a time (i.e., they were unable to form an image in which all four items interacted with one another) although they could image each item separately. As can be seen from the Cermak (1975) task, these patients can form interacting images when only two words are involved and can utilize these images to aid their retrieval. Thus, their limit must be either two or three items in an image. It must be pointed out, however, that the amnesic patients in Cermak's study had to be reminded on each trial of the fact that they had formed an image including both the stimulus and a response. In other words, the procedure itself seemed to be forgotten by the patients even though performance of it seemed to have provided a route to the item's storage in memory.

Some mention should be made of the fact that mediated learning facilitated amnesic patients' retrieval on both of Cermak's (1975) recall tasks (original learning and relearning), but not on the recognition task. A possible explanation may be that recognition provides a more direct access to the response by allowing the patient to match one of the words on the recognition card to one already in storage. Thus, it could be that the mediated cue is bypassed in favor of the more direct route or recognition match. Imagery improves even recognition results, however, so its facilitating effect is all the more impressive.

SERIAL LEARNING

One of the first formal investigations of Korsakoff patients' serial learning was an experiment by Baddeley and Warrington (1970) in which patients were presented with a sequence of 10 unrelated words and were asked to recall them in any order. As can be seen in Figure 3.3, the amnesic patients had grossly impaired recall performance for the early items of the list. As described in Chapter 2, these items are thought to be drawn from LTM. On the other hand, the amnesic patients' recency performance was nearly normal. The ramifications of this outcome will be discussed in the next chapter, but it is important to note here that the only items that seemed to attain LTM status in the amnesics' memory were the first one or two presented.

In an attempt to determine at least one of the factors underlying alcoholic Korsakoff patients' impaired LTM performance, Cermak and Butters (1972) performed an experiment in which the patients were orally presented with a short serial list of eight words. These lists consisted of two words from each of four categories (e.g., animals,

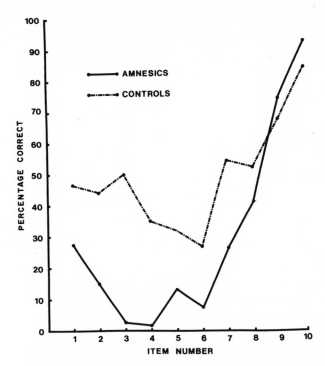

FIGURE 3.3 *The graph illustrates the mean percentage of correct recall of words as a function of the order of their presentation.*

vegetables, professions, and names). Following the reading of the list, the patients were asked immediately to freely recall as many of the words as they could. Some time later, the patients were read a second, similarly constructed list of eight words. However, this time they were told, prior to the reading of the list, precisely what categories were going to be represented and that they would have to recall each word in response to being prompted by a category cue. Under these cued recall conditions, chronic alcoholics with drinking histories that paralleled those of the alcoholic Korsakoff patients, recalled more words than they had under free recall. Conversely, the alcoholic Korsakoff patients actually retrieved fewer words under cued recall than they had under free recall (Figure 3.4). It seemed as if the alcoholic Korsakoff patients could freely "spew-out" the words immediately after they had heard the list, but they could not give each word back under its appropriate category. (Categorized storage is a char-

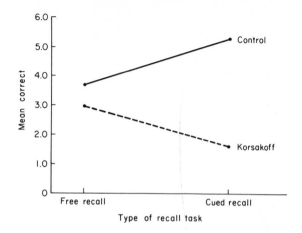

FIGURE 3.4 *The graph illustrates the mean number of correct responses during free recall and cued recall.*

acteristic of the intact LTM system described in Chapter 2.) It appeared as if they were retaining the material in an uncategorized state sufficient for immediate free recall but not for the more complex, cognitive manipulations required in recall from LTM.

The Cermak and Butters (1972) experiment had used lists of words in which each item bore some semantic relationship to at least one other item in the list. It is well known that when no obvious semantic characteristics exist within a list of words, normal adult subjects generally impose some form of subjective organization upon the list in order to retain it (Tulving, 1962). They may, for instance, rehearse the material in chunks of three or more contiguous items, or they may rehearse items together that, for some idiosyncratic reason, seem to the subject to belong together. A technique has been developed by Rundus and Atkinson (1970) that actually allows an experimenter to observe this subjective organization in progress. In this procedure, the subject is asked to rehearse aloud during the presentation of the list. In this way, the extent to which the subject groups items during rehearsal can be monitored. Rundus and Atkinson found that normal adults generally rehearse not only the word presently before them but several words previously presented in the list as well. However, alcoholic Korsakoff patients, as Cermak, Naus, and Reale (1976) discovered, tend spontaneously to rehearse only one word at a time (see

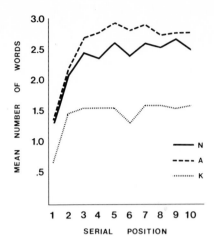

FIGURE 3.5 *The graph illustrates the number of different items rehearsed per rehearsal set by alcoholic Korsakoff (K), alcoholic control (A), and normal control (N) groups as a function of the serial position of the rehearsal set averaged across all list types.*

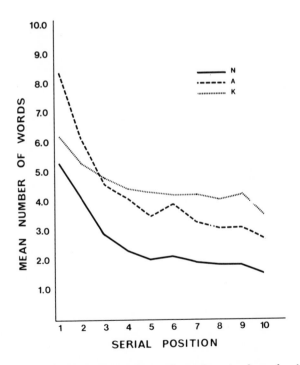

FIGURE 3.6 *The graph illustrates the total number of rehearsals of each word averaged across all rehearsal sets and list types by alcoholic Korsakoff (K), alcoholic control (A), and normal control (N) groups as a function of the serial position of the word.*

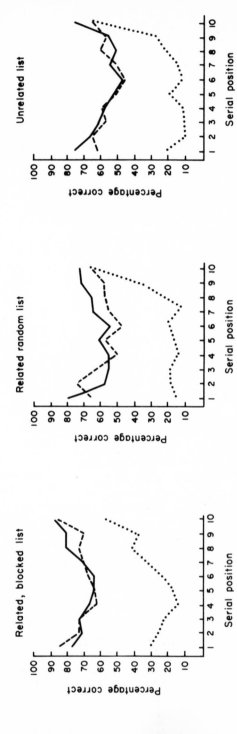

FIGURE 3.7 *The graphs illustrate the percentage of words correctly recalled by the alcoholic Korsakoff (K), alcoholic control (A), and normal control (N) groups as a function of list type and serial position. (N=———; A=———; K=•••)*

Figure 3.5)—that word being the one most recently presented. The consequence of this strategy is that the alcoholic Korsakoff patients actually rehearse each individual word more frequently than either alcoholic or nonalcoholic control subjects (Figure 3.6), but still retain far fewer items than either control group (Figure 3.7). This single-word strategy occurred even when the level of organizational saliency of the list (i.e., the extent to which categories were represented in the list) was increased. Obviously, the alcoholic Korsakoff patients were focusing on no more than one item in the list at a time. In fact, as will be seen in Chapter 5, it now appears that they may even tend to focus on only one "feature" of each particular item at any one time (i.e., the phonemic characteristic of the item).

REMOTE MEMORY

In Chapter 1, it was explained that Korsakoff patients suffer from a sort of "shrinking" retrograde amnesia (Benson & Geschwind, 1967). This total inability to recall recent events, coupled with ever increasing improvements in recall ability as progressively more distant memories are probed, represents an interesting aspect of LTM. Unlike the studies just reported, no new material is introduced to the patient during probes of remote memory. Instead, information that, for most native-born Americans, was learned long ago is being tapped. The fact that nearly normal memory exists for these far distant events bodes ill for a pure, retrieval deficit theory of long-term recall. As the memory disorder becomes progressively more marked for the more recently occurring events, one would have to propose that less and less material is attaining a long-term permanent status. Whether this is due to gradual degeneration of brain function is unknown. However, the availability of so much information from the distant past suggests that at least some important structure of the CNS is intact and functioning in its normal role. At any rate, these remote memories probably form the basis on which the patients function within their daily lives. Their vocabulary, reading skills, socializing skills, etc. are probably those learned in childhood and early adulthood, and must represent skills the patient never loses. The possibility also exists that this information is a part of a nonspecific memory system such as that represented by "semantic" memory.

SEMANTIC MEMORY

Tulving (1972) has suggested that verbal memory might conveniently be divided into two components which he labeled "episodic" and "semantic." He defined *episodic* memory as memory for specific, personally-experienced events, whereas memory for general principles, associations, rules, etc. he defined as *semantic* memory. By now the reader must realize that the alcoholic Korsakoff patients' episodic memory is quite impaired. However, whether their semantic memory is normal or impaired remains undecided. To investigate this system in Korsakoff patients, Cermak, Reale, and Baker (1978) developed a modification of the semantic-memory search procedure originally devised by Freedman and Loftus (1971). This procedure involved presenting the patient with a category name followed by a single letter (e.g., fruit—A) and then asking him to produce, as quickly as possible, a word belonging to this particular category and beginning with this particular letter. Actually, two analyses of search speed were made: one, based upon category searches with single letter cues as just described; the other, requiring a similar search when a category was paired with a descriptive adjective (e.g., fruit—red). These two different types of search were assessed in accordance with the distinction hypothesized by Collins and Loftus (1975) between the two types of semantic memory that could be differentially tapped by these two cue types. One semantic network, which they felt to be organized along the lines of phonemic or orthographic similarity, they termed the *lexicon* or *lexical* semantic memory. The other, organized on the basis of semantic similarities between words, was called *conceptual* semantic memory. The single letter search was designed, therefore, to assess organization of the lexicon, whereas the adjective search assessed the organization of conceptual semantic memory. In the actual experimental procedure, each patient's response time was measured by means of a voice key apparatus that was activated by the presentation of the slide and terminated by the patient's response.

The results (Table 3.2) showed that the alcoholic Korsakoff patients' search of lexical semantic memory was somewhat slower than that of the normal subjects', but not significantly so. On the other hand, their search of conceptual semantic memory (Table 3.3) was dramatically and significantly slower than normal. In fact, the alcoholic Korsakoff patients required, on the average, almost a second longer than normal subjects to search their conceptual semantic memory. From this

TABLE 3.2

Lexical Semantic Memory: Mean Response Time and Number Correct for Korsakoff Patients and Alcoholic Controls

	Korsakoff patients	Alcoholic controls
Mean response time (sec)	4.019	3.788
Mean number correct/80	65.7	69.2

experiment, it was concluded that alcoholic Korsakoff patients' search through semantic memory is impaired when it is based solely on the conceptual features of verbal information, but near normal when it is based primarily on the lexical features of information.

Such a finding raises the possibility that the alcoholic Korsakoff patients' episodic impairment in LTM might actually be a consequence of their semantic memory impairments. In other words, their analysis of incoming information might depend, in part, upon comparing each new item of information to old items of information drawn from conceptual semantic memory. Therefore, an impaired search through conceptual semantic memory might make such comparisons difficult for the Korsakoff patients, so that fewer semantic comparisons would be made. As a result of this reduced search, a lower level of analysis would be performed on the new material. Because the Korsakoff patients appear to possess a nearly normal, lexical search speed, they would be expected to demonstrate a more normal level of phonemic analysis of new information, and indeed, this is exactly what occurs. Consequently, a normal level of retention would also be expected when storage can only be based on a phonemic level of analysis. More will be said about this issue in Chapter 5, where the topic is fully discussed.

Cermak, Reale, and Baker (1978) have also provided evidence for

TABLE 3.3

Conceptual Semantic Memory: Mean Response Time and Number Correct for Korsakoff Patients and Alcoholic Controls

	Korsakoff patients	Alcoholic controls
Mean response time (sec)	4.406	3.701
Mean number correct (perfect score = 80)	67.6	75.8

the converse relationship, namely, that the speed of semantic search may depend upon some aspects of episodic memory. Loftus (1973a,b) presented evidence supporting this possibility by showing that when two consecutive category searches occurred from within the same category, albeit with differing letter cues, the search speed during the second instance was faster than would ordinarily be expected. Apparently, the previous trial's activation of that particular category (an episodic event) serves to "prime" the second search of that category. Loftus reported that this "primed activation" decreases quickly, and even disappears, as soon as two or more intervening items occur between same-category searches. Based on the fact that the alcoholic Korsakoff patients' episodic memory is impaired, it was hypothesized that they would probably show no priming effect, or at least less than would the controls, as the effect seems to depend upon retention of a previous trial. In order to assess this notion, the category–single-letter task was again given to a group of alcoholic Korsakoff patients (Cermak, Reale, & Baker, 1978). The basic procedure was the same as previously described, the only difference being that categories paired with different single letters were repeated within a test session. These same-category trials were separated by either 0, 1, 2, or 3 intervening trials containing items from categories other than the critical repeated category.

The outcome of this task was that the alcoholic Korsakoff patients evidenced absolutely no activation of their lexical semantic memory when the category was "primed" by the immediately prior trial (Table 3.4). The improvement in search speed occurring for the control

TABLE 3.4

Mean Response Time as a Function of the Number of Items Intervening Between Instances of the Same Category

Number of intervening items	Mean response time (sec)	
	Alcoholic Korsakoff patients	Alcoholic controls
0	3.918	3.409
1	3.913	3.710
2	3.998	3.627
3	3.896	3.640
Base	3.952	3.736

patients was simply not present for alcoholic Korsakoff patients. Apparently the "episode" of having just previously searched a particular category was already lost by the time it was probed again, even when the probe occurred on two adjacent trials. This implies that the "preactivation" described by Collins and Loftus (1975) is probably nothing more than normal memory for a recently completed search.

The results from these studies on semantic memory raise two important points in addition to those already cited. First, although the alcoholic Korsakoff patients' search of semantic conceptual memory is slower than normal (indicating perhaps an element of disorganized search), nevertheless, they did respond correctly as often as the normals. This again means that information learned early in life is still present and may be available as a base from which to draw inferences (see Lachman & Lachman, 1979). Second, this remote memory may have become automatic in retrievability, and this feature may be what is retained after the brain damage occurred in the Korsakoff patient. A similar suggestion has been made by Waugh and Barr (1978) in describing why the aged can retain remote memories so well.

MOTOR MEMORY

One other type of memory that borders on becoming automatic once it is learned, is motor memory. Driving a car, riding a bicycle, swimming, all seem to be retrievable at any time with little or no conscious effort, and certainly without the need to verbalize. To evaluate the intactness of motor learning and retention in alcoholic Korsakoff patients, two experiments have been performed: a finger-maze task and a rotary-pursuit task.

In the finger-maze task (Cermak, Lewis, Butters, & Goodglass, 1973), alcoholic Korsakoff patients and their matched alcoholic controls were instructed to find the correct pathway through a four, and then, a six choice-point maze with their index finger. Visual tracking was prevented by imposing a black cloth screen between the patient's body and his hand, which was on the maze. When the end of the maze was reached, the patient's finger was returned to the start position and a new trial began. Trials continued until 2 consecutive errorless trials were achieved, with a limit of 60 trials given to any one patient on either maze.

On this task the alcoholic Korsakoff patients made a total of 93.0

errors before achieving criterion on the four choice-point maze, and 131.1 errors on the six choice-point maze. The controls, on the other hand, made only 25.8 errors and 33.0 errors on the four and six choice-point mazes, respectively. Clearly, the alcoholic Korsakoff patients were impaired in their ability to learn mazes. Probably the correct choices made on one trial were forgotten by the time the next trial began. This intertrial "forgetting" may have been due to an inability to retain a verbal code (e.g., right, left, left) to mediate their learning, an inability to form and retain an image of the maze, or simply to an inability to acquire any motor skill, regardless of the level or type of cognitive mediation involved. To evaluate whether this latter suggestion was a viable possibility, a rotary-pursuit task was administered to the same patients. This task probably does not involve any form of verbal mediation or imagery, but rather seems to be a pure motor skill acquisition task.

To perform the rotary-pursuit task (Cermak *et al.*, 1973), patients had to learn to maintain contact, for 2-sec trials, between a stylus and a small metallic disc on a turntable which was rotating at 45 rpm. The patients were given eight trials a day, four with each hand, for 5 consecutive days. After each trial, the time on and off target was recorded. An improvement score, indicating the difference between the total time on target during the final and initial testing days, was computed for each patient at the conclusion of the final day of testing. Because no significant differences were found between the patient groups on this improvement score, nor for that matter were there any differences in the daily performance, it was concluded that alcoholic Korsakoff patients were not impaired in the acquisition of a pure motor skill. Their impairment on the finger maze tasks must have involved some problem with cognitive (i.e., verbal) mediation.

To summarize this chapter on LTM, it can be stated that alcoholic Korsakoff patients' long-term recall of newly learned responses is almost nil. However, some trace must remain beyond the time when it is available for free recall as relearning is usually faster than original learning. Mnemonic devices do seem to facilitate learning and retention to some extent, but only temporarily, and at a level far below normal. the patients' semantic memory organization seems to be intact, although search of at least the conceptual component of this memory is slow and may be limited, which suggests a possible cause for their impaired cognitive analysis of incoming information (to be discussed in Chapter 5). "Automatic" retrieval, particularly for over-learned remote memories, appears normal and may represent the most intact memory system exhibited by these patients. In fact, retrieval from this system may be what enables alcoholic Korsakoff patients to perform well on IQ tests and to function in a limited fashion in their daily lives. New motor tasks may also be learned and retained if the tasks do not involve the use of verbal mediation to integrate their various components.

4

Short-Term Memory

The vast majority of research on the short-term memory (STM) ability of alcoholic Korsakoff patients has made use of the distractor technique (for review, see Chapter 2). However, tests involving the serial recency effect and a form of a memory "scanning" technique have also been employed. The impetus for the investigation of this area of memory actually developed from the frequent clinical observation that, despite the fact that these patients repeatedly forget the tester's name minutes after hearing it and are unable to recall any day-to-day events, they can, nevertheless, follow instructions and answer questions. In addition, amnesics usually have a normal or nearly normal digit span. These observations all suggest the hypothesis that amnesic patients may have a normal STM in the presence of a very impaired long-term memory (LTM). Indeed, this independence hypothesis led Baddeley and Warrington (1970) to perform a series of STM tasks with an amnesic population that consisted of alcoholic Korsakoff patients as well as patients with other etiologies (e.g., herpes encephalitis). The first of these was a serial-learning task in which the recency portion of the recall curve came under scrutiny. This emphasis on recency stemmed from the belief that the latter portion of the list is held in STM (see Chapter 2).

RECENCY IN SERIAL LEARNING

In their first study of STM, Baddeley and Warrington (1970) presented each of six amnesic patients (four of whom were alcoholic Korsakoff patients) with a serial list of 10 nouns at the rate of 1 word every 3 sec. Following the visual presentation of the last word, each patient was signaled to try to recall, in any order, the 10 words he or she had just seen. The patient received 10 such lists, as well as 10 other serial lists for which recall was delayed by a 30-sec retention interval. Baddeley and Warrington reasoned that if amnesics have a normal STM, this should be reflected in a normal recency effect on at least the immediate recall trials. On the other hand, recall of the primary portion of each list (or of the entire list when recall was delayed) should be deficient because this material would be in LTM, a storage system known to be impaired for all amnesic patients.

The results of this serial-learning experiment (Figures 4.1 and 4.2)

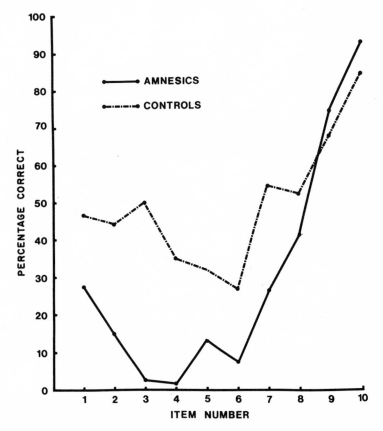

FIGURE 4.1 *The graph illustrates the mean percentage of correct recall of words under immediate recall conditions as a function of their order of presentation to amnesic and control groups.*

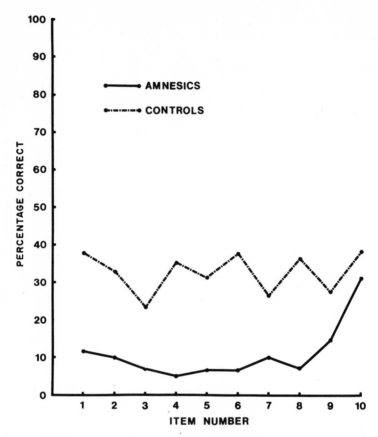

FIGURE 4.2 *The graph illustrates the mean percentage correct recall of words under delayed recall conditions as a function of their order of presentation to amnesic control groups.*

support Baddeley and Warrington's thesis extremely well. The amnesics do show a marked recency effect that borders on being completely normal when recall is immediate. However, the early portion of the amnesics' curve is impaired, as is almost their entire delayed recall curve. Although these findings suggest that amnesics have intact STM capacities, three points should be made about these results:

1. Since, as noted in Chapter 2, the most recent portion of a long list of words is generally recalled first by patients, the alcoholic Korsakoff patients' recency performance, like their digit-span scores, may represent the normal "capacity" of STM, but does not necessarily

indicate that amnesics have a normal ability to hold material in STM in the face of interference.

2. The recency portion of the amnesic patients' curve is not quite normal, as evidenced by positions 6, 7, and 8. This "slipping" recency might represent a faster rate of information loss from STM for alcoholic Korsakoff patients than for normals.

3. Baddeley and Warrington's results were not replicated by Cermak, Naus, and Reale (1976) in their experiment on the relationship between recall and rehearsal.

As will be remembered from Chapter 3, Cermak *et al.* (1976) had included a recall test at the end of each trial of their rehearsal strategy task. As this free recall (Figure 3.6) was also of a serial list, it was comparable to the Baddeley and Warrington experiment. On this task, a strong recency effect was found, especially for the unrelated word lists. However, the slope of this recency effect was much steeper than that found by Baddeley and Warrington. In fact, only the last one or two items were ever recalled by the patients. Therefore, recall fell to approximately the same level as that for the middle of the list. This result suggests that alcoholic Korsakoff patients may suffer not only from an accelerated rate of decay from STM but also from an impaired storage capacity.

DISTRACTOR TASK RECALL

As was stated previously, the most frequently employed paradigm for studying the amnesics' rate of forgetting has been the distractor technique. In the same article referred to in the previous section, Baddeley and Warrington (1970) reported the results of administering the distractor task to amnesics as a further means of exploring the STM–LTM dichotomy. In their procedure, the patients were shown three, three-letter words for 4 sec. Then, the patients were presented with a three-digit number from which they were asked to count backwards for anywhere from 0 to 60 sec. Recall was signaled by the presentation of a red asterisk.

The results can be seen in Figure 4.3. It is evident from this figure that the amnesics and the normal controls do not differ significantly in their rate of forgetting—even after 60 sec of distraction. This finding is most surprising in view of Milner's (1966, 1970) ob-

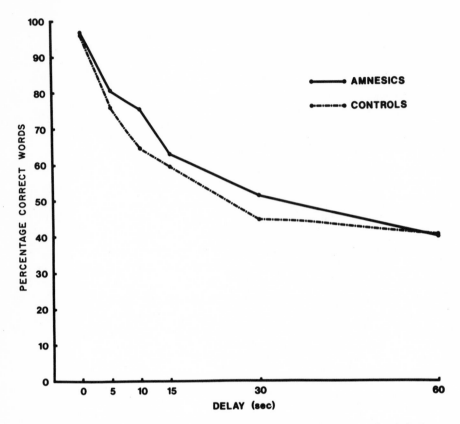

FIGURE 4.3 *The graph illustrates the short-term retention of word triads by amnesic and control groups after varying periods of distraction.*

servations that the amnesic patient H. M. had to depend upon continuous recirculation (i.e., rehearsal) to retain any information. The slightest distraction had a disastrous effect upon H. M.'s attempt to retain new materials.

Except for this single report by Baddeley and Warrington, all other studies employing the distractor technique with alcoholic Korsakoff patients have reported severe impairments in this amnesic population. Cermak, Butters, and Goodglass (1971), as well as Kinsbourne and Wood (1975), found dramatic deficits using consonant trigrams such as S,Z,K (Figure 4.4), word triads such as *flower—ship—house* (Figure 4.5), or single words (Figure 4.6) as the to-be-remembered materials. The alcoholic Korsakoff patients perform normally at the zero-second

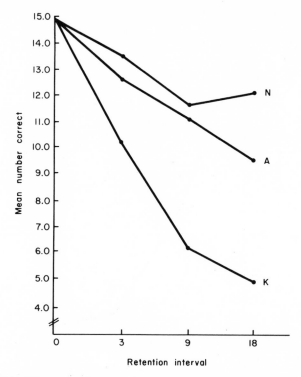

FIGURE 4.4 *The graph illustrates the mean number of correct responses for alcoholic Korsakoff (K), alcoholic control (A), and normal control (N) groups during the CCC recall condition.*

delay interval, but thereafter their decay functions are much steeper than those of control subjects. In fact, after only a 9-sec delay, the alcoholic Korsakoff patients are able to recall little of the previously presented materials, regardless of the sensory modality (visual, auditory) or type of stimulus material employed.

Recall from STM is normally affected not only by the amount of time that passes between presentation and retrieval, but also by the amount of interference that is present during retention (Chapter 2). Two experiments were therefore designed to determine whether the alcoholic Korsakoff patients lost material from STM as a function of time, or whether these patients were more susceptible than normal individuals to the effects of interference. In the first investigation (Cermak & Butters, 1972), the patients' STM capacities were assessed under both high and low proactive interference (PI) conditions. The

55

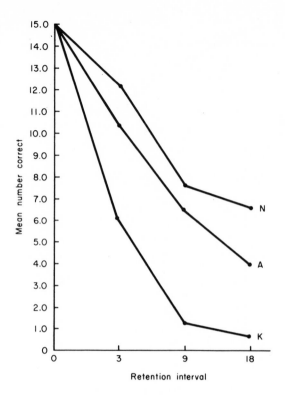

FIGURE 4.5 *The graph illustrates the mean number of correct responses for alcoholic Korsakoff (K), alcoholic control (A), and normal control (N) groups during the word-triad recall condition.*

distractor technique was again employed with two types of verbal material, consonant trigrams (CCCs) and word triads (WWWs), as the to-be-remembered stimuli. The experimental trials were administered in blocks of two with a 6-sec intertrial interval. By varying the similarity of the material presented on the first and second trials of each block, it was possible to analyze the effects of high and low PI conditions. Specifically, the first trial involved the presentation of a CCC (low PI condition) on half the blocks and the presentation of a WWW (high PI condition) on the other half. A WWW was always presented on the second trial of each two-trial block. On the first trial of each block, the patient always counted backwards for 9 sec before attempting recall; on the second trial, the patient counted backward

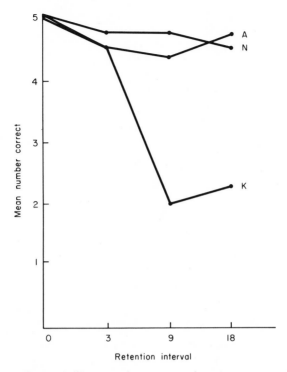

FIGURE 4.6 *The graph illustrates the mean number of correct responses for alcoholic Korsakoff (K), alcoholic control (A), and normal control (N) groups during the one-word recall condition.*

for either 3, 9, or 18 sec before attempting recall. There was a 1-min rest interval between each block of trials.

The patients' recall performance on the second trial of the two-trial block is shown in Figure 4.7. Both the alcoholic Korsakoff patients and the alcoholic controls had more difficulty under high versus low PI conditions, but the proportion of recall decrement between the low and high PI conditions was significantly greater for the alcoholic Korsakoff patients than for the control group. At 9 sec, recall from low to high PI conditions dropped 53% in Korsakoff patients and only 23% in the control group. At 18 sec, the decrement was 40% in alcoholic Korsakoff patients and 14% in controls. These results provided strong evidence that the alcoholic Korsakoff patients were more sensitive than the control group to the effects of PI.

A similar finding occurred when the to-be-remembered verbal

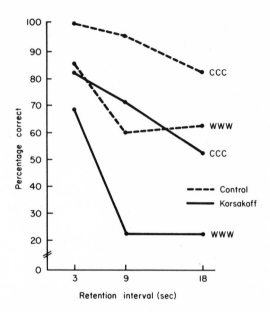

FIGURE 4.7 *The graph illustrates the percentage of word triads (WWW) recalled following high and low proactive interference (PI) conditions after retention intervals of 3, 9, and 18 sec. High PI conditions are after word triads (WWW) and low PI conditions are after consonant triads (CCC).*

materials were given either in mass or distributed presentation (i.e., with either a 6-sec or a 1-min rest interval between succeeding trials). On the basis of research with normal individuals, it had been observed that less PI was generated with distributed than with massed practice (i.e., presentation). Therefore, it was hypothesized that if, indeed, the alcoholic Korsakoff patients were abnormally susceptible to interference, then they should show a significant improvement in recall with distributed practice.

The alcoholic Korsakoff patients and the alcoholic control group did show better recall with distributed rather than massed practice on both WWWs and CCCs. But, as expected, the difference in performance between distributed and massed practice was greater for the alcoholic Korsakoff patients than it was for the alcoholic control group. The proportion of recall decrement (from distributed to massed practice) for WWWs was 76% for alcoholic Korsakoff patients and only 32% for the control group. When CCCs were employed, the decrement was 30% for the alcoholic Korsakoff patients and only

11% for the control group. It is also interesting to note that alcoholic Korsakoff patients, under distributed practice conditions, performed as well as, or better than, the control group did under massed conditions.

One issue that was raised in Chapter 2 concerning the distinction between the effects of interference in LTM and STM was that the interference that produces forgetting in LTM is semantic, whereas that in STM is phonemic. Given this notion, and some of the findings that have thus far been presented concerning the processing skills of alcoholic Korsakoff patients, the next step was to determine whether the massed versus distributed and high versus low PI results might indicate that the alcoholic Korsakoff patients were more susceptible than normal individuals to the effects of the phonemic interference occurring during an STM retention interval. Evidence supporting this possibility was provided in a study reported by DeLuca, Cermak, and Butters (1976). In this experiment, the nature of the distractor task performed during the retention interval was varied, rather than the nature of the to-be-remembered stimulus materials. In one condition, patients were asked to perform a note-tracking task (nonverbal distraction) during the retention interval; in another, they were asked to shadow consonant trigrams presented through headphones (acoustic distraction); and, in a third, they were told to scan a page of words looking for words belonging to a given target category (semantic distraction). It was discovered (Figure 4.8) that shadowing consonant trigrams interfered with the alcoholic Korsakoff patients' retention of words, but did not interfere with the control group's retention. The nonverbal distraction (note tracking) did not interfere with either group's verbal retention. This result (i.e., that the phonemic distractor interfered with the alcoholic Korsakoff patient's retention) implied that the alcoholic Korsakoff patients must have been more susceptible to the effects of this type of interference than was the control group. This susceptibility may have been due to the patients' complete dependence upon their phonemic analysis of the words—a thesis that will be further explored in Chapter 5. The semantic distraction interfered with both groups' retention; however, as the distractor stimuli were related phonemically as well as semantically to the memoranda, they very nearly eliminated the alcoholic Korsakoff patients' memory traces.

In a later investigation, Cermak, Reale, and DeLuca (1977) reported that the alcoholic Korsakoff patients could retain verbal material even

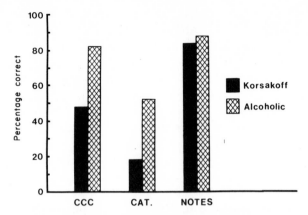

FIGURE 4.8 *The graph illustrates the percentage of correct responses by both groups following 20-sec delay intervals filled with repeating consonant trigrams (CCC), scanning for same category (CAT.), or note discrimination (NOTES) distractor activities.*

after relatively long delay intervals (at least 40 sec) when absolutely no distraction occurred (Figure 4.9). It seemed that the alcoholic Korsakoff patients had some sort of recirculatory mechanism that they could use to retain the material when no distraction prevented its use. However, identical verbal material dissipated quite rapidly across retention intervals varying from 5 to 40 sec as soon as any type of verbal distraction did occur (Figure 4.9). Evidently, whatever recirculatory mechanism these patients use (e.g., one based on their phonemic processing), it is capable only of strengthening their memory traces enough to permit immediate retrieval. The traces lose strength rapidly once verbal interference is interjected.

Cermak, Reale, and DeLuca also uncovered an interesting characteristic of alcoholic Korsakoff patients' "nonverbal" retention. Unlike their verbal retention, the alcoholic Korsakoffs' memory for nonverbal stimuli dissipated over time (0–40 sec) even when no distraction occurred (Figure 4.9). It seemed as if these patients did not possess any mechanism for the rehearsal of nonverbal material. As it is supposed that normals use some form of imagery to retain nonverbal materials, it may be hypothesized that alcoholic Korsakoff patients do not use this technique. Cermak, Reale, and DeLuca also reported that any nonverbal distraction during the retention interval would immediately result in the disruption of the alcoholic Korsakoff patients' retention of nonverbal materials (Figure 4.9). This loss occurred

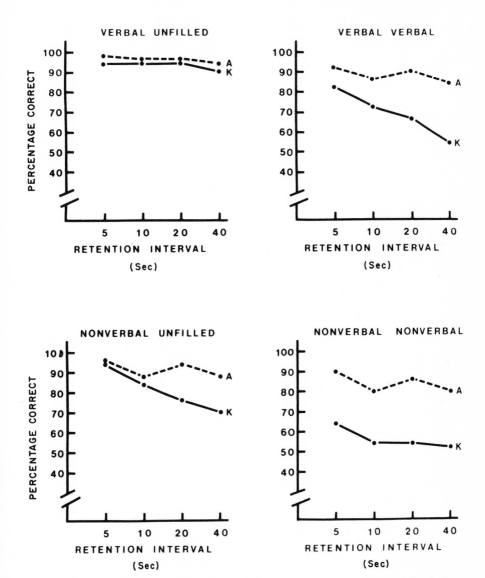

FIGURE 4.9 *The graphs illustrate the percentage of correct responses by both alcoholic Korsakoff (K) and alcoholic control (A) groups on the two verbal and the two nonverbal recognition tasks after conditions of no distraction or verbal/nonverbal distraction during the retention interval.*

abruptly, rather than gradually as had been the case for verbal retention in the face of verbal distraction.

On the basis of the evidence reviewed, it appears that alcoholic Korsakoff patients are impaired on distractor tasks employing verbal or nonverbal material as the to-be-remembered stimuli. However, the processes underlying these verbal and nonverbal STM deficits may differ. In the case of verbal retention, alcoholic Korsakoff patients may depend upon a relatively weak recirculatory mechanism that can be easily disrupted by interference from similar material. In the case of nonverbal retention, no real recirculatory mechanism seems to be available to these patients, and consequently memory impairments exist with or without distraction. As alcoholic Korsakoff patients are known to be "capable" of utilizing imagery when so instructed (e.g., Cermak, 1975; Huppert & Piercy, 1976), it must be concluded that when left to their own devices, these patients, unlike normal adults, simply do not spontaneously employ imagery to aid their retention of nonverbal material.

RATE OF RETRIEVAL FROM SHORT-TERM MEMORY

Once it became evident that the rate at which alcoholic Korsakoff patients lose incoming verbal information was far more rapid than normal, it seemed reasonable to investigate whether other aspects of their STM system were similarly affected. The most logical candidate for assessment was the rate at which alcoholic Korsakoff patients could retrieve information known to exist in storage. The paradigm that was selected as being appropriate for this investigation was one developed by Sternberg (1966), in which a short list of letters (2–6) is presented to the patient followed immediately by a probe letter. The patient's task is to decide whether or not the probe letter was a member of the just-presented set and to indicate this decision by depressing either a predesignated yes key or no key. These keys are programmed to terminate a timer that is activated by the presentation of the probe. In the actual experiment (Naus, Cermak, & DeLuca, 1977), it was determined that the alcoholic Korsakoff patients "knew" the set of letters prior to the probe by the fact that they responded correctly almost 100% of the time. However, their rate of responding was slower than that of the alcoholic control group in two respects (Figure 4.10). First, the slope of the line, plotting reaction times as a

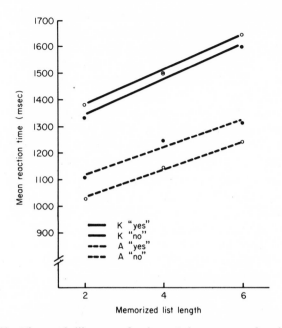

FIGURE 4.10 *The graph illustrates the slope of the mean reaction time as a function of memorized list length for "yes" and "no" responses for alcoholic Korsakoff (K) and alcoholic control (A) groups.*

function of the serial position of the target stimulus, was steeper for the alcoholic Korsakoff patients than it was for the control group. This indicated that they were scanning the memorized list more slowly than the control group. Second, the intercept of the same line at the Y axis was higher for the alcoholic Korsakoff patients than for the alcoholic control group. This indicated that each individual stimulus in the list was being checked against the probe item more slowly by the alcoholic Korsakoff patients than by the control group. Both these measures suggested that alcoholic Korsakoff patients must be retarded in their speed of retrieval relative to normal rates.

Another speed of retrieval task performed with these same patients resulted in essentially the same conclusion. Glosser, Butters, and Samuels (1976) presented pairs of digits dichotically to alcoholic Korsakoff patients and a control group. The subjects were instructed to press a response key if the dichotic pairs met certain specified criteria. When the interpair interval was 1.2 sec, the alcoholic Korsakoff patients could detect the presence of a single digit in one channel (e.g., they could detect "9" when it was presented to the right ear), but were impaired in their detection of specific combinations of numbers (e.g., in detecting the simultaneous presentation of "10" to the left ear and "9" to the right ear). However, when the interpair interval was increased from 1.2 sec to 2 sec, the alcoholic Korsakoff patients performed normally on this task. Apparently, alcoholic Korsakoff patients simply needed more time than normal individuals to "read out" the material held in STM. When the pairs of stimuli occurred too rapidly, each digit interfered with this readout from STM, and the patient's performance was impaired.

In summary, both the rate of information loss and the rate of retrieval from STM have been shown to be different for alcoholic Korsakoff patients than for control groups. The alcoholic Korsakoff patients lose the material more rapidly than control groups largely because they are more sensitive to the effects of interstimulus and distractor task interference. The alcoholic Korsakoff patients' rate of retrieval of information known to be in STM is also slower than normal. Although it is true that the alcoholic Korsakoffs' storage capacity is within the normal range (as evidenced by their normal digit-span performance), their STM is still deficient because of the rapid loss of materials and slow speed of retrieval.

The two experiments just discussed actually border on testing retrieval from sensory memory, but the intervals of presentation and retrieval were not nearly as rapid as those generally used in the sensory memory experiments outlined in Chapter 2. Few, actual sensory-memory paradigms have been adapted for use with alcoholic Korsakoff patients, however, those in existence will be reported in the next section of this chapter.

SENSORY MEMORY

The fact that so few sensory memory experiments have been performed with alcoholic Korsakoff patients may be explained by the difficulties inherent in the procedures themselves. An unpublished study exemplifies these difficulties when the Sperling technique was adapted for use with alcoholic Korsakoff patients. In this procedure two types of recall are tested, the whole report and the partial report. When the whole report procedure is used, the subject sees 3–12 letters briefly (usually for about 250–500 msecs), and is then required to recall as many items as possible from that array. Normal subjects usually recall about 4.3 items. When partial recall is required, the subject always sees 12 letters (three rows of four columns) and is signaled, after the offset of the array, for recall of one of the three rows. Normal subjects generally can recall 3–4 letters from any of the rows, indicating that more material is available to them immediately after presentation than they are able to utilize during the act of retrieval.

When this paradigm was used with alcoholic Korsakoff patients, it was discovered that 500 msec was too rapid a presentation for the patients. Even with the whole report procedure, the patients were rarely able to detect even one letter. Increasing the time to 1000 msec, and in some instances to 1500 msec, resulted in the recall of about 3.5 items by all the patients. This performance was still less than normal, but was approximately the same as that achieved by the alcoholic control patients when the presentation was 500 msec. Consequently, individual presentation rates, determined with the whole report condition, were used when attempting to introduce the partial report procedure.

Prior to introducing the partial report task, each patient was trained to discriminate among three widely disparate tones. Following this training, they were taught a tone-row, paired association (i.e., high tone/top row, medium tone/middle row, and low tone/bottom row). The alcoholic Korsakoff patients could master these associations, but their skill broke down completely when an attempt was made to transfer them to the Sperling task. The alcoholic Korsakoff patients were instructed to fixate the center of the array and to wait for the tone to inform them which row to recall. However, even when the tone coincided with the offset of the stimulus array (i.e., no delay), the patients consistently recalled either nothing or letters from a preferred, rather than the requested, row. Several of these patients seemed to attend to the top row and would correctly recall items from that row most of the time; others chose the middle row; and some chose no row at all. Although the alcoholic Korsakoff patients knew that a particular row was being requested, they continued to perseverate their preferred tendency. A number of other investigators (e.g., Oscar-Berman, 1973; Talland, 1965) have also reported that the alcoholic Korsakoff patients' inability to shift sets is very detrimental to their performance on a variety of conceptual and perceptual tasks.

One instance in which a sensory memory experiment was successfully conducted with alcoholic Korsakoff patients can be seen in the work of Oscar-Berman, Goodglass, and Cherlow (1973), who found that these patients had elevated visual-recognition thresholds for both words and patterns (i.e., to insure correct identification of a word or pattern, a longer stimulus duration had to be used for the alcoholic Korsakoff patients than for the normal group). Oscar-Berman *et al.* also reported that alcoholic Korsakoff patients were more prone to visual masking than were normal control groups. The masking of an initial visual stimulus by the presentation of a second could be demonstrated with relatively long interstimulus intervals when alcoholic Korsakoff patients served as subjects. These findings suggested to the investigators (Oscar-Berman *et al.*, 1973) that alcoholic Korsakoff patients are slow in their analysis of a stimulus' visual features and, therefore, are very limited in the amount of feature analysis they can accomplish within any given time period. In view of this impairment in the processing of information in sensory memory, it should not be surprising to find that Korsakoff patients have additional difficulties with more complicated analyses of verbal and nonverbal materials.

SHORT-TERM MOTOR MEMORY

As it had been shown that alcoholic Korsakoff patients had deficits in both verbal and nonverbal STM, it seemed likely that they might also be impaired in their ability to retain a motor movement. What needed to be determined, however, was whether such a deficit, if it did exist, would be secondary to their verbal memory deficit. This determination was necessary because so many of our motor-memory acts can normally be mediated by some sort of verbal code. To assess the role of verbal mediation in short-term motor memory, a task involving the retention of a simple motor movement with, or without, verbal distraction was performed (Cermak & Uhly, 1975).

A group of 10 alcoholic Korsakoff patients and 10 alcoholic patients were positioned before the center of a 50-in board to which a carpenter's sliding tape measure had been attached. The experimenter blindfolded the patient, put the patient's hand on the apparatus, pulled the slide out to a predetermined distance, and then returned it and the patient's hand to the starting position. The patient was then asked to try to replicate the distance by extending the slide to the same position. Following 10 nondelay trials of this sort, a delay interval of either 10 or 20 sec was introduced between the target demonstration and the patient's attempt to replicate the distance. During this interval, the patient either counted backwards by two's or used his index finger to perform an alternating tapping task. It was hypothesized that if the alcoholic Korsakoff patients used some form of verbal mediation (such as retaining approximate length estimates), then verbal distraction should cause more forgetting than the "motor" distraction. However, if the patients used some other means of retaining distance (e.g., visual or proprioceptive imagery), then either both types of distraction should be equal, or the motor distraction should produce more forgetting. The results, which are shown in Figure 4.11, revealed a motor memory deficit for the alcoholic Korsakoff patients following 10- or 20-sec delays filled with either type of interference. This deficit was not simply due to a motor impairment or an inability to replicate the experimenter's movement because these patients were unimpaired when no delay intervened between the target demonstra-

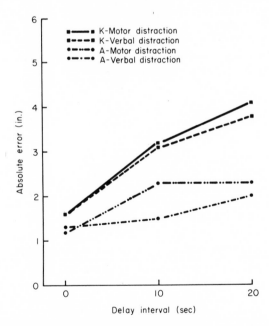

FIGURE 4.11 *The graph illustrates the mean absolute error for alcoholic Korsakoff (K) and alcoholic control groups (A) after no delay and following 10- and 20-sec delays filled with either verbal or motor distraction.*

tion and replication. As verbal and motor distractions proved to be equally interfering, the alcoholic Korsakoff patients' observed deficit in motor memory could not be wholly attributed to deficits in verbal mediation and retention. It appears, then, that the alcoholic Korsakoff patients' STM impairments extend not only to verbal and nonverbal retention, but to motor-movement retention as well. Unfortunately, these results do not leave much firm ground on which to build any type of therapeutic memory program. The alcoholic Korsakoff patient's short-term storage is so susceptible to the effects of interference that these patients can only retain the immediate present.

5

Encoding Deficits

At approximately the same time that much of the research reported in the preceding chapters was being performed, a change in emphasis was developing among theories of normal information processing. This change was primarily motivated by the publication of several investigations that seemed to question the very defining characteristics of the memory stores first described in Chapter 2 and then relied upon in subsequent chapters. In particular, distinctions based on differential capacities, differential utilization of codes, and differential life spans came under fire.

It will be remembered that differential capacity had been a major distinction between the three stores, with Sperling (1960) finding a limit of about four items that could be retrieved from immediate memory (IM), Miller (1956) estimating short-term memory capacity at 7 ± 2 items (which could be extended by chunking), and Waugh and Norman (1965) suggesting that long-term memory capacity was infinite. Problems with these limitations began to emerge when both Dick (1969) and Clark (1969) found that some categories of information (e.g., color) could be retained in immediate memory more successfully than others (e.g., letters). In fact, they found nearly perfect recall of color position from any row of a stimulus array when poststimulus cues were given as late as 2 sec after the array presentation. Taylor (1969) found a similar effect for figures. Attempts to estimate short-term memory (STM) capacity also found highly variable results as a function of the type of material retained. Baddeley (1970) and Murdock (1972) found capacities of only 2–4 unrelated words, whereas Craik and Masani (1969) found subjects could accurately reproduce strings of up to 20 such words when they tried to form sentences from them.

In light of these data, the box-model system was hard pressed to firmly delineate the capacity limits of each subsystem of memory.

Regarding the type of code utilized, Sperling (1960) and Treisman (1964) had each proposed that material in immediate memory is coded in purely "physical" terms; Conrad (1964) and Baddeley (1966) had shown that material in STM is coded acoustically; and most theorists (including Waugh & Norman, 1965) argued that material held in long-term memory (LTM) is coded primarily in semantic terms. However, in 1959, Moray demonstrated that some highly relevant words (especially one's own name) can be selected from among unattended items during shadowing experiments, which suggests that some semantic (or at the very least, phonemic) analysis takes place prior to an item's entry into STM. Treisman (1964) and Aaronson (1967) have also presented similar findings, each suggesting that several levels of analysis might exist during initial processing, and that these analyses probably occur at an extremely rapid rate. In the area of STM, Levy (1971) and Peterson and Johnson (1971) have demonstrated that STM can hold acoustic or physical (articulatory) features of information, and Kroll and his colleagues (1970) have demonstrated that STM utilizes the visual aspects of verbal information. At the other end of the spectrum, Shulman (1970) has presented persuasive evidence to indicate that semantic encoding also occurs in STM. After these findings were made, the position that encoding characteristics distinguished one store from the other could no longer be maintained.

Finally, even the bastion of differential life spans, or rates of forgetting, as a means of differentiating the three stores fell before conflicting evidence. Neisser (1967) had argued that the icon lasted about 1 sec or less, but Posner (1969) found evidence of its existence for up to 1.5 sec. Then Murdock (1971), Phillips and Baddeley (1971), and Kroll et al. (1970) found estimates of 6, 10, and 25 sec, respectively. Estimates were even longer for recognition memory of briefly presented pictures (Haber, 1970; Shepard, 1967). In the area of STM, Kintsch (1970) showed retention extending over as many as 20 items in a paired-associate learning task, whereas free-recall and probe paradigms had shown much faster rates of information loss (Waugh & Norman, 1965). Physiological psychologists presented evidence to suggest that consolidation from STM to LTM can be disrupted in anywhere from a few seconds (Chorover & Schiller, 1965), to a few days (Pearlman, Sharpless, & Jarvick, 1961), or to a few weeks (Flexner, Flexner, & Stellar, 1963), depending upon the nature of the task and the disrupting agent. Thus, the length of time an item can stay in STM became much harder to delineate, and the "normal" rate of forgetting from each system became impossible to determine.

In reaction to this wave of disparate evidence, both Cermak (1972) and Craik and Lockhart (1972) made proposals suggesting that theories that emphasized differential storage systems had to be discarded. In their place, they proposed that memory theorists should concentrate on the initial encoding operations that are performed and should attempt to determine whether retention might not be a function of the type of encoding. Craik and Lockhart (1972) further suggested that the type of interference effective in preventing retrieval at any given time might be primarily dependent upon the manner in which the to-be-recalled item was represented in memory. Phonemic interference might effectively block only material represented on the basis of its phonemic features, while not effectively preventing retrieval of semantically represented traces. The reverse would also be true: Semantic interference should not prevent retrieval of phonemically represented material, but might well interfere with the retrieval of semantically encoded information.

Craik and Lockhart (1972) further proposed that analysis of an item's semantic, rather than phonemic, features would ensure more effective storage and, consequently, a more durable representation in memory. Phonemic analysis, in turn, was felt to provide a longer lasting representation than physical analysis. This concept of a hierarchy of processing stages was referred to by Craik and Lockhart as "depth of processing," in which greater "depth" implied a greater degree of semantic or cognitive analysis.

Memory has gradually come to be viewed as a sort of by-product of the extent, or depth, to which an item was analyzed (i.e., the greater the extent of analysis, the stronger and more durable the memory trace produced by it). The amount of interference present in a memory task was still felt to be dependent on the number of similarly encoded (i.e., analyzed and stored) traces in memory, but now it was proposed that the manner in which an item was initially analyzed would determine its chances of being able to overcome this interference.

Craik and Lockhart further pointed out that stimuli can also be retained through the continual recirculation of information at any one level of processing. This type of processing, which they called *maintenance processing*, simply repeated the analyses already carried out. Although this rehearsal kept the item active in memory and available for recall, Craik and Lockhart proposed that it did nothing to strengthen the item's memory representation. *Elaborative processing,* on the other hand, involved continual creation of deeper analyses of the item, thus improving its later retrieval probability through a strengthening of its representation. To the extent that elaborative processing was utilized, increased study time improved retention; but when maintenance processing was relied on, increased time did not appear to add to the strengthening of an item in memory (see also Cooper & Pantle, 1967; Stoff & Eagle, 1971).

Based on this emerging theory, a great deal of research has now been performed with alcoholic Korsakoff patients to determine the extent of their analytic (i.e., encoding) difficulties. As these patients had been shown to have little or no ability to learn new material, it made sense to ask whether they might have an information processing deficit of such a magnitude that it could account for their memory disorder. If this were so, then not only would their difficulty be more fully understood, but further support for the encoding theory of memory would be obtained.

The first indication that alcoholic Korsakoff patients' memory deficit might in any way be related to a difficulty in their encoding operations occurred in an experiment reported by Cermak and Butters (1972) and was described in Chapter 4. In this experiment, a list of eight words, containing two words from each of four different categories (animals, professions, vegetables, and names), was read to each patient. Following the reading of the list, the patients were simply asked to recall the words in any order (free-recall condition), and the number of words they correctly recalled was recorded. The patients were then told that they would receive a second list of eight words, and, as the words were drawn from specific categories, that they would be asked to recall the words category by category when so prompted by the experimenter. Patients were always told what these categories would be prior to the reading of the list. Although cueing by category did improve the control subjects' recall, the alcoholic Korsakoff patients actually retrieved fewer words under cued recall than under free recall. This suggested the possibility that alcoholic Korsakoff patients had not employed a semantic encoding strategy to the same extent as the control group. Consequently, the alcoholic Korsakoff patients were able to recall the words on a rote basis in the free-recall condition, but their performance deteriorated when they were called on to recall the words on the basis of the semantic features of each word.

This evidence in favor of the hypothesis that alcoholic Korsakoff patients have an encoding deficit conflicted with a report by Warrington and Weiskrantz (1971), who found that cued recall was superior to free recall for both alcoholic Korsakoff and control patients. There was, however, one significant difference in the procedures of the two studies. Whereas Cermak and Butters had tested recall immediately after the reading of the list, Warrington and Weiskrantz had delayed their recall for 1 min. By replicating both procedures, Cermak, Butters, and Gerrein (1973) found that the two results were not really in conflict at all. Rather, the length of the retention interval was found to interact with the type of recall task in determining the probability of recall (Figure 5.1). The immediate recall results replicated the findings of Cermak and Butters (1972), whereas the delayed recall results were similar to those of Warrington and Weiskrantz. It can be seen that the alcoholic control group were slightly aided by cueing, but

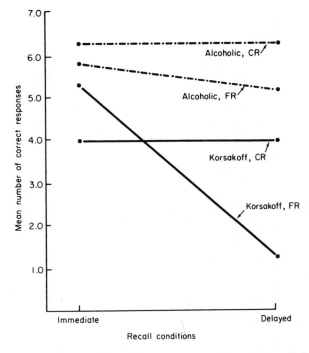

FIGURE 5.1 *The graph illustrates the mean number of words recalled correctly during recall (CR) and free recall (FR) under immediate and delayed recall conditions.*

their immediate and delayed performances were almost identical. In comparison, the alcoholic Korsakoff patients' immediate and delayed recall were identical for cueing, but their free recall performance deteriorated after only a 1-min delay.

These findings suggest that perhaps the alcoholic Korsakoff and alcoholic patients differ in their spontaneous use of semantic encoding strategies. The control patients seem to have employed, spontaneously, a semantic encoding strategy under both the cued and the free-recall conditions—a tactic that resulted in equal, immediate and delayed, recall performance. The alcoholic Korsakoff patients seemed to employ such strategies only when so instructed by the examiner, such as on the cued recall conditions. When left to their own devices (i.e., free recall), the alcoholic Korsakoff patients appeared to rely upon rote memory, which is of course based upon a less sophisticated, acoustic-encoding strategy. Thus, the alcoholic Korsakoff patients' significant decrement in performance between immediate and delayed free recall might have been a reflection of their inability to spontaneously employ semantic encoding to aid their retention and retrieval.

This latter hypothesis was tested in a series of experiments by Cermak, Butters, and Gerrein (1973) that were designed to investigate the extent to which alcoholic Korsakoff patients could encode information under both prompted and unprompted conditions. As the previous experiment had shown that cueing facilitated the alcoholic Korsakoff patients' delayed recall, it was felt that these patients might be capable of at least some semantic encoding. To determine more precisely the extent of their ability to categorize information, three procedures previously used to assess the encoding abilities of normal subjects, were adapted for use with alcoholic Korsakoff patients.

In the first experiment, the patients were cued for the recall of specific words from a serially presented list. The cues consisted either of a rhyme of the to-be-recalled word, or the name of the category of which the to-be-recalled word was an exemplar. Bregman (1968) had proposed that the facilitating effects provided by these cues could be taken as being indicative of the degree of encoding achieved by the subject. If only rhyming cues aided his recall, then the subject had apparently encoded only the acoustic dimension of the word and not the semantic dimensions. If both types of cues aided recall, then the subject must have encoded both these features of the word. In the actual experiment each patient was told, prior to the reading of the list of words, the cue type to be used throughout the list. The words were then presented on cards with the probe, or cue words, bracketed by question marks as the signal for recall. Each patient was tested using both types of cues, but only one type of cue was used at a time.

It turned out that the rhyming and category cues were equally effective for both groups when the to-be-recalled item and its cue were separated by only one or two intervening items (Figure 5.2). However, with longer delays (three or six items) between presentation and cued recall, group differences appeared. In these instances, the facilitating effects of category cues appeared to decay more rapidly for the alcoholic Korsakoff group than for the alcoholic control group. Because materials encoded on sophisticated levels (i.e., through semantic encoding) are supposed to be more permanent and less subject to decay (Baddeley & Dale, 1966; Tulving, 1970), the sharp decline in the facilitating effects of the category cues seen in alcoholic Korsakoff patients again seemed to indicate a deficiency in their original semantic encoding of the to-be-recalled words.

In the second experiment of this series, the encoding of the associative dimensions of words was investigated. Bahrick (1969) had shown that when subjects are unable to remember a word (e.g., chair), their

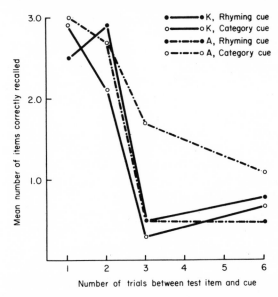

FIGURE 5.2 *The graph shows the mean number of correct responses for alcoholic Korsakoff (K) and alcoholic control (A) groups as a function of the type and delay of the probe.*

recall can be aided if they are cued with an associate (e.g., table) of the word. The probability that the associate will aid retrieval of the to-be-remembered word has been shown to be directly correlated with the strength of association between the two words. This cueing value of associates is probably due to some implicit encoding of the associate at the same time the to-be-recalled word is originally processed (Underwood, 1965). It was hypothesized that if alcoholic Korsakoff patients automatically engage in this type of associative encoding, then providing them with associates of the to-be-recalled words should facilitate their recall ability as it does for normal individuals.

The procedure involved presenting six paired-associate word combinations to the patients at a rate of one pair every 2 sec. After all the pairs had been presented, the patient was shown only the first member of each pair and asked to remember the word originally paired with that word. If the patient failed to recall the correct response, the experimenter said, "Here's a hint," and presented an associate of the correct response. Then, the patient was given the opportunity to try again to recall the desired response. As all the associative cues had a .27 probability of eliciting the correct response, any increment in the patient's probability of recall beyond this .27 level was taken as evidence that the associate had been implicitly encoded the first time the patient had seen the to-be-recalled word.

The results showed that the control patients recalled more words than the alcoholic Korsakoff patients without cueing, but the probability that the item would be retrieved following associative cueing was essentially the same for both groups of patients. The probability that an alcoholic Korsakoff patient would be aided by the cue was 50 percent (23 percent above what was expected by chance), whereas the alcoholics were aided in 61 percent of the cases in which they could not recall a word. This finding indicates that the degree to which alcoholic Korsakoff patients implicitly encode primary associates of a to-be-remembered word is essentially normal.

This experiment demonstrated that alcoholic Korsakoff patients do encode associative semantic features of words. Consequently, the only explanation for their memory impairment seemed to lie in the "extent" to which they encode information along these dimensions. In other words, it now appeared that, under the appropriate instructional conditions, alcoholic Korsakoff patients seem to be capable of semantic encoding. However, when they were not so instructed they seemed to prefer to rely on their encoding of the acoustic dimensions of words.

If this is true, then it would not be so surprising that the alcoholic Korsakoff patients' STM decays rapidly, or that it is highly susceptible to interference, as information encoded solely on the basis of its acoustic features decays more rapidly than materials encoded semantically.

In order to assess this refined hypothesis (i.e., alcoholic Korsakoff patients may be capable of semantic encoding but prefer to rely on less sophisticated categorizations) a false recognition test (Underwood, 1965) was used. In this task a 60-word stimulus list was shown at the rate of one word every 2 sec to the patient. The patient's task was to detect any repetitions presented within the list. Although the list actually contained repetitions, it also contained several words that were acoustically identical (i.e., homonyms such as *bear* and *bare*), highly associated (e.g., *table* and *chair*), or synonymous (e.g., *robber* and *thief*). Whenever the patient indicated that a homonym, an associate, or a synonym was a repetition, it was scored as a false recognition. If the patient had preferred to encode only the acoustic features of the words, then he would have falsely recognized some of the homonyms as being repetitions. Associative false recognitions would have indicated that an associative level of encoding had been achieved, and synonym false recognitions would have indicated that a still more sophisticated semantic level of encoding had been accomplished. In other words, the type of errors made by the alcoholic Korsakoff patients would be indicative of the extent to which they normally encoded information.

The results showed that the alcoholic Korsafoff patients falsely recognized more homonyms and associates as being repetitions than did the control group. On the other hand, they made as many correct identifications as the control group and made no more synonym, or neutral-word false recognitions. These results would suggest that alcoholic Korsakoff patients encode words on acoustic and associative dimensions, but do not encode the semantic dimensions of the words to an extent that would allow the rejection of acoustically identical, or highly associated words. The fact that all the preceding experiments have demonstrated that alcoholic Korsakoff patients are capable of encoding semantically when instructed to do so (as in the cueing studies), supports the belief that they fail to spontaneously encode the semantic dimension of words when left to their own devices.

Still further evidence for the existence of this phenomenon was provided by Cermak and Moreines (1976), who employed a paradigm in which similar features were to be detected rather than "falsely" recognized. This test, first introduced by Cermak and Youtz (1974), required that the patient listen to a list of words read at a constant rate and indicate (a) when a word was repeated (repetition condition), (b) when a word rhymed with a previous word (phonemic condition), or (c) when a word belonged to the same category as a preceding word (semantic condition). The patient did not have to indicate which previous word was the match, nor did he have to explain the rationale for his choice. All he had to do was to indicate when the target word occurred. Memory for particular features was then monitored by plotting the number of correct choices as a function of the number of words intervening between the initial and probe members of each pair. As no verbal response had to be made, Broca's aphasics were also given this task so that comparisons could be made between this group, known to have severe verbal difficulties, and the alcoholic Korsakoff group.

The results (an example of which can be seen in Figure 5.3) revealed that alcoholic Korsakoff patients consistently performed worse on the semantic task than the alcoholic control group and approximately the same as the control group on all other tasks, except where four items intervened during the phonemic task. Thus, it appeared that although alcoholic Korsakoff patients may have been capable of retaining verbal information in working memory on the basis of a phonemic code, they failed to do so when the capacity of this system was exceeded, or when they were asked to make semantic judgments based on this code. We shall now turn to a later series of experiments that confirm this finding.

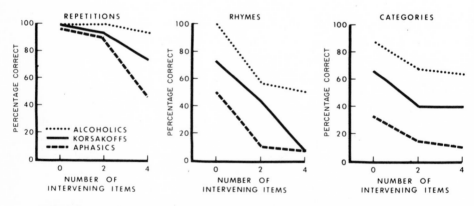

FIGURE 5.3 *The graphs illustrate the percentage of target words correctly identified by each group on each of the three tasks as a function of the number of intervening words presented at a word-per-sec rate.*

The studies reported in Chapter 3 and 4 demonstrated that alcoholic Korsakoff patients had an increased sensitivity to proactive interference (PI), and the present chapter has shown an impairment in these patients' encoding strategies. However, the relationship between these two deficits has not been clearly stated. At least two descriptions of the relationship would be plausible. For example, the two deficits might be totally independent of one another and may represent two separate deficits in the total alcoholic Korsakoff syndrome. Alternatively, the patients' increased sensitivity to PI may result from their lack of analysis of the semantic dimensions of information.

To test this latter hypothesis, Wickens' (1970) "release-from-proactive-inhibition" technique was adapted for use with alcoholic Korsakoff patients (Cermak, Butters, & Moreines, 1974). Using a modification of the Peterson distractor technique, Wickens had discovered that the PI generated by the presentation on several consecutive trials of material from the same class of information could be released by the introduction of material from a new class of information. This finding was interpreted to mean that the extent of interference during STM recall is largely a function of the subject's ability to differentiate words in memory on the basis of their semantic features. Evidently, when a subject encodes material differentially, this material is stored independently and does not interfere with the retrieval of other types of material. It was predicted that if the alcoholic Korsakoff patients' increased sensitivity to interference is related to their lack of semantic encoding, then the amount of PI release demonstrated by these patients should vary with the encoding requirements of the verbal materials. It was anticipated that alcoholic Korsakoff patients would demonstrate normal PI release when the verbal materials involved only rudimentary categorizations (e.g., letters versus numbers); but that when the stimulus materials involved more abstract semantic differences (e.g., taxonomic differences such as animals versus vegetables), the alcoholic Korsakoff patients would show far less PI release.

Wickens' procedure employs an STM distractor technique in which the subjects are tested in blocks of five trials. Information from the same category is presented on the first four trials of a five-trial block. On the fifth trial, however, information from a different category of material is presented. For example, if consonant trigrams (CCCs such as R,Q, F) are presented on the first four trials, a three-digit number (NNN such as 813) might be shown to the subject on the fifth trial. This test procedure can also utilize taxonomic (categorical) shifts. For example, on the first four trials, word triads (WWWs) composed of animal names (e.g., dog—elephant—monkey) may be shown to the subject, then on the fifth trial, the taxonomic category of the three stimulus words is shifted to vegetables (e.g., lettuce—squash—potatoes).

Normal performance on these tasks is well-documented and has also been replicated in the authors' laboratory with alcoholic control subjects. Figure 5.4 shows the release that occurs for the control patients in the alphanumeric (CCC–NNN) paradigm. In the experimental (shift) condition, performance decreases for the first four trials, but after the shift of materials on the fifth trial, there is a large improvement in performance (i.e., a release from inhibition). No such improvement occurs for the control (nonshift) condition.

Figure 5.5 shows the performance of the alcoholic control group on a release-from-PI task involving taxonomic shifts (e.g., animals to vegetables or vice versa). The results are similar to those for the alphanumeric paradigm. When the taxonomic shift in materials occurs (experimental condition), there is, again, a release from the PI, as evidenced by the improvement in recall.

Figure 5.6 presents the results for the alcoholic Korsakoff patients when the alphanumeric shift condition was presented to them. When the letter–number shift occurred on the fifth trial (experimental con

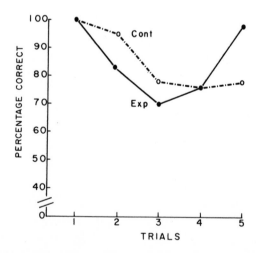

FIGURE 5.4 *The graph illustrates the probability of recall following an alphanumeric shift for alcoholic controls.*

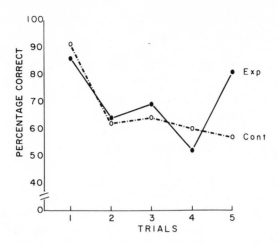

FIGURE 5.5   *The graph illustrates the probability of recall following a taxonomic shift for alcoholic controls.*

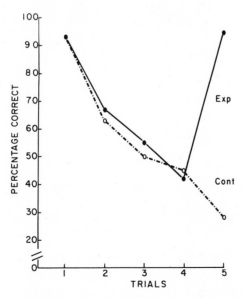

FIGURE 5.6   *The graph illustrates the probability of recall following an alphanumeric shift for alcoholic Korsakoff patients.*

dition), the alcoholic Korsakoff patients demonstrated a complete release from PI. Their recall performance on the fifth trial of the experimental condition was just as good as their performance on the first
trial of the same condition. As demonstrated previously by Warrington and Weiskrantz (1971) and by Cermak and Butters (1972), the alcoholic Korsakoff patient can retain verbal information in a normal
manner if the learning conditions are arranged to minimize the effects
of PI. Their performance on the first four trials illustrated an increased sensitivity to PI. Although there was a significant decrement in
the control patients' recall during the first four trials, the decrement
was much greater for the alcoholic Korsakoff patients. Apparently, interference accumulates at a faster rate for alcoholic Korsakoff patients.

Figure 5.7 shows the PI release results for the alcoholic Korsakoff
patients when different taxonomic (animal–vegetable) categories were
used. An accelerated decline in recall over the first trials was again evident. However, the important finding in this instance was that the alcoholic Korsakoff patients did not improve on the fifth (shift) trial of the
experimental condition. As the alcoholic control patients do show a
release under the taxonomic conditions, the Korsakoff patients' inability to do so must reflect some underlying deficit characteristic of
these patients. This suggests that perhaps an inability to encode
verbal information along semantic dimensions could explain the

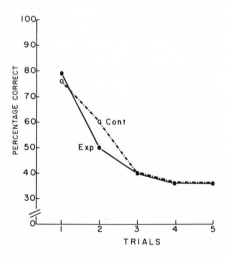

FIGURE 5.7 *The graph illustrates the probability of recall following a taxonomic
shift for alcoholic Korsakoff patients.*

alcoholic Korsakoff groups' failure on the taxonomic shift experiment. To perform the alphanumeric shift, the patient had only to encode the difference between letters and numbers, but in the taxonomic shift paradigm, the patient had to encode the semantic or categorical features of the particular words. If alcoholic Korsakoff patients did not encode along such semantic dimensions, then the PI accumulating during the block of five trials would probably not be specific to any one category (animals, vegetables), and therefore a shift of categories would have no effect. Thus, it appeared that alcoholic Korsakoff patients' lack of semantic encoding both maximized the amount of accumulating PI and prevented the release from this interference.

At this point, it can be said with some degree of confidence that alcoholic Korsakoff patients' information processing must be deficient. It is apparent that they analyze each individual item of information to a lesser extent than normal individuals, contrast each item with other information in permanent memory less readily than normal individuals, and use inappropriate strategies for rehearsal and chunking of information. All these factors seem to contribute to their overall anterograde memory deficit. The next question to be asked is whether or not techniques designed to improve processing might lead to improved retention in alcoholic Korsakoff patients.

The first technique chosen for testing was one reported in detail by Craik and Tulving (1975) and also used extensively by Jenkins (Hyde & Jenkins, 1973; Till & Jenkins, 1973; Walsh & Jenkins, 1973). This procedure attempts to direct the patient's analysis of incoming information so that he or she is forced to analyze the semantic features of the information, rather than just the phonemic features. Patients are not told that they will have to remember anything, rather they are simply instructed to analyze each word on the basis of the particular feature indicated by the nature of the question. The rationale is that the higher the level of analysis the individual is required to perform on a word, the greater will be the probability that he will remember the word on an unexpected recognition test. Questions are designed to necessitate processing on one of three levels: (a) a shallow, orthographic level (e.g., a question about the word's physical appearance, such as "Is this in upper case letters?"); (b) an intermediate phonemic level (e.g., "Does this rhyme with _____?"); or (c) a higher, semantic level (e.g. "Does this fit into the sentence: _____ _____ _____?"). To each question the patient is required to respond either yes or no by pressing the appropriate response key. After the entire series of questions is finished, patients are given a recognition test to see how many words they can recognize as having appeared in the series.

In the actual experiment (Cermak & Reale, 1978), each patient was asked to answer 60 questions, including 20 sentence, 20 rhyme, and 20 orthographic questions. All question types were divided evenly into yes and no responses. The unexpected recognition task at the end of the questioning session consisted of a typewritten sheet containing 180 words (i.e., the 60 list-words plus 120, unrelated filler nouns). It was discovered that alcoholic Korsakoff patients could respond to the questions without error at a nearly normal rate relative to that of the alcoholic control group (Figure 5.8). However, their recognition performance fell far below the control group on all but the orthographically remembered words (Figure 5.9). This was due

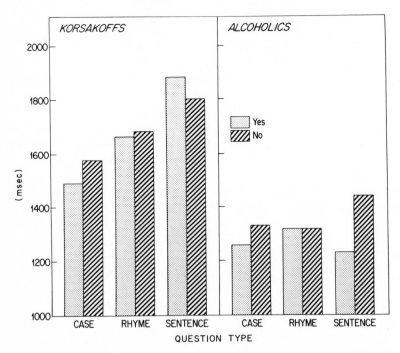

FIGURE 5.8 *The graph shows the initial decision latency (msec) for alcoholic Korsakoff and alcoholic control groups as a function of the type of question asked about the word.*

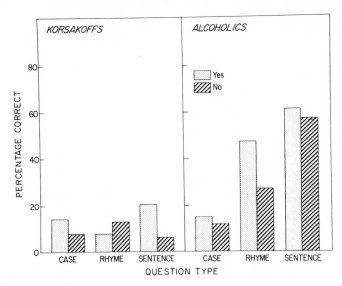

FIGURE 5.9 *The graph illustrates the percentage of words correctly recognized on a recognition task by alcoholic Korsakoff and alcoholic control groups as a function of the type of question initially asked about the word.*

largely to the fact that the alcoholic Korsakoff group recognized a similar number of words at all levels of analysis. No greater benefit to later retention accrued for the words that were analyzed at the "deeper" levels than had accrued for words analyzed at "shallow" levels. It was possible, however, that the nature of the recognition task had produced these results by so overwhelming the patients that they merely scanned the list briefly, circled a few words, and gave up. In order to obviate this situation, a forced recognition test was administered.

The same materials, questions, and procedure from the preceding experiment were used in the forced recognition test, but the 180 words appearing on the recognition test were now presented in groups of three (two filler words and a target item). The patient was instructed to circle one word from each of the 60 triads. A different question regarding each word was asked of those alcoholic Korsakoff patients who had participated in the prior experiment. This was done even though no patient remembered having ever performed this type of task before, and would not, of course, have remembered that an unexpected recognition test was going to occur.

Figures 5.10 and 5.11 show that the results of this experiment

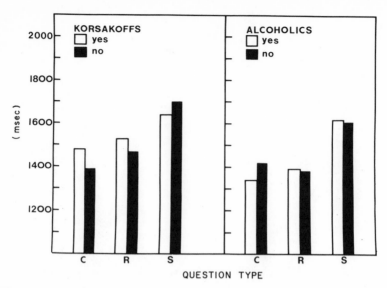

FIGURE 5.10 *The graphs illustrate the initial decision latency (msec) for alcoholic Korsakoff and alcoholic control groups as a function of the type of question (C = case, R = rhyme, S = sentence) asked about the word.*

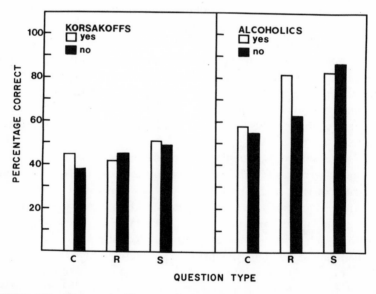

FIGURE 5.11 *The graphs illustrate the percentage of words correctly recognized by alcoholic Korsakoff and alcoholic control groups as a function of the type of question (C = case, R = rhyme, S = sentence) initially asked about the word.*

very nearly duplicated those of the previous experiment, despite the change in recognition procedure. Instructions to alcoholic Korsakoff patients to perform semantic analysis did not result in greater retention levels than did lower levels of processing. It was decided at this point that perhaps the sentence questions used in the first two experiments did not provide enough structure for the alcoholic Korsakoff patients to utilize in storing and retrieving the words. Consequently, it was decided to use two other forms of semantic query. One form depicted the category of the test word; the other asked a specific question that could only be answered by the test word.

Fifty-six words were chosen in such a way that four different types of questions could be asked of each. Two questions were of the same variety as those used in the preceding experiments, namely, sentence and rhyme questions. The other two were directed more specifically toward defining the target words. One question was of the type "Is this a _____?" in which the blank was filled with the name of a category. The other question asked, "Does this _____ have _____?". The first blank was again the name of a category, but the second blank included a defining characteristic of the word. Examples of these questions, which were called "category" and "specific marker" questions, are given in Table 5.1. It was felt that category questions might define the words more fully than sentence questions and that specific marker questions might define them yet further.

The form of recognition task used was again the forced choice recognition task. Words were arranged in groups of three, with each triad containing one correct and two incorrect words, making a total of 56 triads. The results (Figures 5.12 and 5.13) again replicated those of the preceding two experiments. The alcoholic Korsakoff patients responded somewhat more slowly than the alcoholic control patients, but their pattern of response was the same. Also, the alcoholic Korsakoff patients recognized far fewer words than did the alcoholic patients

TABLE 5.1
Examples of Questions and Answers

Type of question	Example of question type	"Yes" answer	"No" answer
Category	Is this a flower?	rose	CHAIR
Specific marker	Does this animal have stripes?	ZEBRA	lion

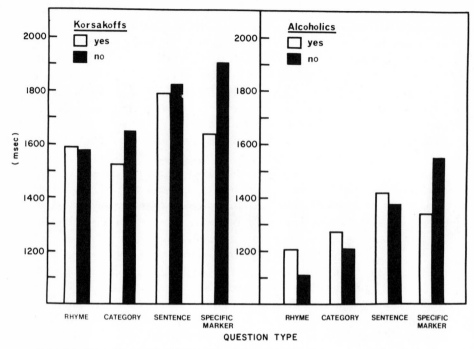

FIGURE 5.12 *The graphs illustrate the initial decision latency (msec) for alcoholic Korsakoffs and alcoholic controls as a function of the type of question asked about the word.*

under all conditions and without differences in recognition as a function of question type. On the other hand, the control group recognized more marker, sentence, and category words than rhyme words, and marginally more marker words than sentence or category words.

Despite the fact that the questions used in this experiment had been designed to direct the patient toward analyzing specific semantic characteristics of the words, no improvement in retention occurred for the alcoholic Korsakoff patients. Thus, it simply had to be concluded that even when these patients are forced to encode in a specific manner and to circle an appropriate number of responses, the probability of their retaining semantically analyzed information is no better than their retention of information analyzed on the basis of ordinarily less robust (e.g., phonemic) features within the confines of this paradigm. It became obvious that if an effect of semantic analysis were to be demonstrated with alcoholic Korsakoff patients, the basic paradigm

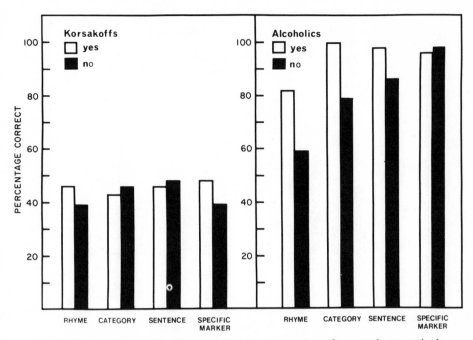

FIGURE 5.13 *The graphs illustrate the percentage of words correctly recognized by alcoholic Korsakoff and alcoholic control groups as a function of the type of question initially asked about the word.*

would have to be modified considerably. Therefore, the list of words was divided into several short lists, each followed by a recognition trial. The experiment differed from the basic task in that the patients were no longer given 60 words and questions in a continuous order, followed by a 180-word recognition test. Instead, they were asked just 12 questions about 12 words, followed by a 36-word "free" recognition test. This procedure was repeated five times until all 60 words had been queried and tested for recognition. Each of the 12-item lists contained 4 words queried by an orthographic question, 4 queried by a rhyme question, and 4 by a sentence question. In addition, two yes and two no questions were asked within each of these three conditions. This manipulation put the alcoholic control group's performance at ceiling for all levels of analysis. However, as the usual pattern of recognition responses was by now so well documented, the test was still conducted and reported as a within-subject design, using only the alcoholic Korsakoff patients.

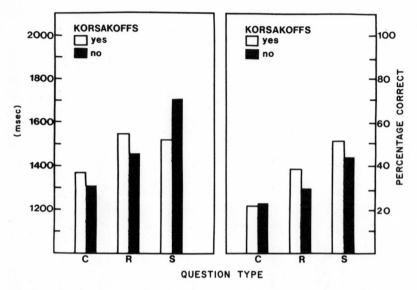

FIGURE 5.14 *Initial decision latency (msec) and proportion of words correctly recognized by alcoholic Korsakoff patients as a function of the type of question (C = case, R = rhyme, S = sentence) asked about the word.*

Figure 5.14 depicts the reaction-time results using this procedure with alcoholic Korsakoff patients. The figure combines the results from the five response time and recognition subtests given to the patients. An analysis of variance performed on the time to respond to each question revealed a significant difference between question types and, in addition, there was now a significant Question-type–Response-type Interaction. The combined results of performance on all five recognition tests showed that a significant effect between question types finally occurred for the alcoholic Korsakoff patients because, at last, they recognized significantly more sentence words than either rhyme or orthographic words, and marginally, more rhyme than orthographic words.

The results of this final experiment somewhat redeemed the rationale behind using the Craik and Tulving procedure to study the relationship between information analysis and retention, as it demonstrated that alcoholic Korsakoff patients' retention of, at least, a brief list of material can be affected by the level of analysis they perform on each word. Under these conditions of abbreviated list retention, the differential effects of physical, phonemic, and semantic analysis can be seen to have the same relative results for alcoholic Korsa-koff patients as they do for normal individuals. This strengthens the contention that differential levels of analysis can "produce" differential probabilities of retrieval, as the type of analysis demanded by the instructions must have been responsible for the improvement. Had no improvement occurred, or had it occurred equally for all levels of analysis, then this "production" hypothesis would not have received any support.

It must also be pointed out that the pattern of the alcoholic Korsa-koff patients' speed of analysis, following different types of query, was consistently normal. Semantic analyses always took longer than phonemic, which in turn took longer than physical. The only instance in which the alcoholic Korsakoff patients took significantly longer than the control group to analyze the words was in the experiment requiring categorical comparisons. However, this finding is consistent with the Cermak *et al.* (1978) demonstration that alcoholic Korsakoff patients are impaired in the rate at which they can search "conceptual" semantic memory. It could be, as was suggested earlier (Chapter 3), that their impairment in the speed of analyzing categorical features is a reflection of their impairment in the search speed through this type of semantic memory.

In summary, it appears that alcoholic Korsakoff patients' recognition memory for verbal information can be affected by the level to which they process that information, at least under some conditions. This, in turn, lends support to previous contentions (e.g., Cermak, 1977; Cermak & Moreines, 1976) that alcoholic Korsakoff patients' anterograde amnesia stems, at least in part, from a preference *not* to perform semantic analyses of to-be-retained verbal information. Had we been unable to demonstrate, under any circumstances, that instructions to perform semantic analysis improved these patients' retentive abilities, then we would have had to discontinue proposing that deficiencies in informational analysis account, in part, for these patients' memory deficits. However, as such instructions did improve retention, such hypothesis remains tenable and deserves further investigation.

The levels-of-processing framework for investigating normal memory has not existed without controversy during its short life-span. Indeed, the notion of "levels" has served not only to stimulate and direct an enormous amount of research, but it has also provided other theorists with an excellent foil. There are at least two areas of research within which these latter theorists have been able to supply data, forcing revision of the original "levels" formulation. The first of these areas concerns the relationship of the retention test to the original learning situation. The second reexamines the basic kernel of the theory that semantic encoding necessarily leads to better retention than phonemic encoding, which, in turn, affords better retention than physical feature encoding.

Tulving (1970, 1979) was among the first to propose that there might be an interaction between the encoding operations present at input and the circumstances (i.e., cues) present at retrieval. He proposed that the "level" of encoding is not as important as is the degree of similarity between input and output cues. His encoding specificity principle (1970) postulated that semantic encoding would only be useful if retrieval was attempted in the presence of these same semantic cues. If it were not, then the semantic encoding might actually prove debilitating. For instance, a subject could be cued at retrieval by a phonemic cue when the word was originally encoded in the presence of a category cue. Under these retrieval conditions, having encoded the word phonemically should produce a higher potential for retrieval than having encoded it semantically. Thomson and Tulving (1970) showed this to be true, at least for weak versus strong associative cues in a modified P-A task.

Interestingly enough, it was Fisher and Craik (1977) who provided the most direct test of this thesis, using the now standard "levels" paradigm. They showed that retention levels were highest when the same type of information was used as a cue for a word at retrieval as had been used in the input question for analysis. Thus, rhyme cues were more effective than semantic cues when the subject had been asked at input whether the to-be-remembered word rhymed with another word. However, Fisher and Craik also found that rhyme encoding followed by rhyme cueing gave lower levels of performance than did semantic encoding followed by semantic cueing. Furthermore, they found that this advantage of semantic encoding over phonemic encoding increased as the retrieval cue was made more compatible with the encoded trace. Thus, they proposed that the levels of processing notion had to be coupled with the encoding specificity hypothesis in order to explain results of this type. However, "level" of processing was still the dominant determiner of the probability of retrieval. Tulving (1979) would argue this point, but, to date, it appears to be mostly a matter of theoretical emphasis, as paradigms seem to be devisable to favor either alternative.

Bransford and his colleagues (1977, 1979) also seem to favor the encoding specificity hypothesis. In a series of experiments, these authors found that when the retention test is semantic, semantic learning leads to better performance than phonemic learning. However, when the retention test is phonemic, a rhyming task performed during learning leads to better retention than a semantic task. Furthermore, they found that subjects given orthographic encoding instructions (i.e., to decide whether or not a particular letter of a word is capitalized) performed better than those receiving semantic encoding instructions on a word recognition task (i.e., the subject was to decide if the word had the same or a different letter capitalized). Naturally, when the recognition task involved a semantic search, semantic encoding gave superior results. As a general pattern, Bransford *et al.* did find somewhat better retention on their semantic tasks than on the others. However, they felt that this was because the subjects had had more experience with this type of task. They did not attribute this superiority to anything inherent in the nature of semantic encoding per se.

In accordance with Tulving's findings, Nelson (1979) has reported that interference occurs during P-A learning, even when words share only similar letters between lists. This was an especially powerful effect when the letters shared were the ones in the initial positions, and the effect became most dramatic when long time intervals existed between the presentations of lists containing these similar words. On the basis of the "levels" framework alone, such orthographic analysis would be predicted to dissipate rapidly. Further evidence for retention of such orthographic properties as long as 1 year later comes from the work of Kolers (1975, 1979), who found that subjects could remember whether a sentence they had read had been printed upside down. Also, as Kolers points out (1979), people often remember where on a page they have read something, and frequently even remember the color of the binding of a particular book. All of these remembrances are incidental to our semantic understanding and retention of the material.

From these studies one is forced to conclude both that: (*a*) deep processing does not necessarily lead to optimum performance, as the nature of the retention task may interact with the probability of retrieval; and (*b*) shallow levels of analysis do not necessarily produce shorter life spans than the deeper levels of analysis. These two modifications have been acknowledged by Craik (1979) in his analysis of the continuing development of the levels-of-processing framework, and they have been partially absorbed into the framework for studying encoding deficits of alcoholic Korsakoff patients.

One of the ways in which these notions were incorporated into studies with alcoholic Korsakoff subjects has been to redo the Craik and Tulving procedure using the same task, except that the patients were cued either with the same question used at input, or a new one from the same level, or one from a different level (see Fisher & Craik, 1977, for the procedure). It was discovered that the only beneficial condition for the alcoholic Korsakoff patients was when the same semantic cue was given at both input and output. This suggests that the encoding specificity principle might hold for alcoholic Korsakoff patients, at least on the semantic level of processing. In order to follow this notion further, the Thompson and Tulving (1970) procedure was also adopted for use with alcoholic Korsakoff patients.

In this procedure, the patients were given a list of 12 word pairs consisting of a capitalized to-be-remembered (TBR) word and an associated word that was printed above it in lowercase letters. The patient was told to memorize each TBR word, but to also pay attention to the small related word, as it might help him remember the TBR word. After the words were presented, the patient was given a sheet on which were printed the 12 cue words with a blank next to each and told to write down the associated TBR words. This procedure was repeated five times, and five different input–output relationships were investigated: (a) S–S, in which a strongly associated cue word occurred at input and again at output; (b) W–W, in which the same weakly associated cue word occurred at input and output; (c) S–W, in which a strong associate was presented at input, but a weak associate at output; (d) W–S, in which a weak associate was present at input, but a strong one at output; and (e) 0–0, in which no cues were given.

The results, shown in Table 5.2, are extremely interesting. Unlike normals, alcoholic Korsakoff patients were not so much affected by encoding specificity (as evidenced by the poor W–W recall) as they were by the presence of a strong associate at retrieval. That this was most obvious in the S–S condition, argues for some retention of the encoding conditions, but apparently only when they reinforce something already existent in semantic memory (see also Cermak, Reale, &

TABLE 5.2

Percentage of Target Words Correctly Recalled

Patient group	Condition				
	S–S	W–W	W–S	O–O	S–W
Alcoholic Korsakoff	57	14	33	29	7
Alcoholic	91	75	63	57	24

Baker, 1978) and not when a new associate is formed. Indeed, the W–W condition elicits worse scores than no cues at all, and S–W exceeds W–W, demonstrating the potential of high-associate elicitation of TBR words (although W–S results are still no better than 0–0).

From this, one could conclude that alcoholic Korsakoff patients' retention can be improved by providing semantic contexts of TBR material, but only if the semantic context at input and output is identical and does not represent "new or creative learning." That is to say, if the semantic context simply reestablishes remote learning, it may be facilitating, but when it necessitates a cognitive reorganization of a subject's semantic network for purposes of retaining an episodic event, the outcome is abysmal. This same cognitive sluggishness has been seen in the limited extent to which alcoholic Korsakoff patients spontaneously analyze, organize, and rehearse verbal input, and is reflected throughout their attempts to retrieve information.

Before turning to a description of alternative theoretical approaches that attempt to explain alcoholic Korsakoff patients' verbal-memory disorder, the present, information-processing approach will be applied to these patients' visuoperceptive deficits. We shall return to the thesis developed here, at the conclusion of Chapter 7 on alternative theories, in which comparisons are drawn among the various theoretical approaches to the study of amnesia.

___6___

Depth of Encoding
and Visuoperceptive Deficits

As noted in Chapter 1, the alcoholic Korsakoff patient has, in addition to his severe amnesia, significant visuoperceptive difficulties. Talland (1965) reported a wide array of such deficits, including failures in locating hidden words and embedded figures, errors in line tracing, abnormal thresholds for apparent movement, and difficulty in producing reversals of the Necker cube. Studies from our laboratory have frequently noted the alcoholic Korsakoff patients' difficulties on digit-symbol substitution and embedded figures tasks (Butters & Cermak, 1976; Butters, Cermak, Montgomery, & Adinolfi, 1977; Glosser, Butters, & Kaplan, 1977; Kapur & Butters, 1977). Our interest in these perceptual disorders has been twofold: (*a*) to determine the perceptual processes (e.g., visual scanning, contour analysis) contributing to the visuoperceptual defects of these patients, and (*b*) to investigate whether the same types of information-processing deficits (limited encoding) that contribute to their memory impairments might also play a role in their perceptual problems.

ANALYSES OF THE ALCOHOLIC KORSAKOFF
PATIENT'S DEFICITS ON THE DIGIT-SYMBOL TEST

Glosser, Butters, and Kaplan (1977) have questioned whether the alcoholic Korsakoff patients' deficits observed on digit-symbol tasks represent visuoperceptive deficits or simply a motor retardation due to chronic alcoholism. They administered a modified version of the WAIS digit-symbol test to 12 alcoholic Korsakoff patients, 12 chronic alcoholics, 12 nonalcoholic individuals, and 11 patients with right-hemispheric brain damage (RBD). These RBD patients were in-

96

cluded because they were known to have a wide array of visuoperceptive deficits (e.g., Warrington, 1969; Warrington & James, 1967), and because chronic alcohol abuse is often associated with neuropsychological deficits similar to those of RBD patients (Parsons, 1975). The test employed two sets of nine symbols that differed in their verbalizability. Nine symbols were known to evoke verbal associations with little difficulty, whereas the other nine (nonverbal) symbols had very low association values. Each set of symbols was then paired with a single-digit number as on the WAIS. These pairings were each administered under two different conditions. In the standard administration, the task was identical with the WAIS digit-symbol test. The patient was presented with four rows of numbers and had to copy (substitute) the symbol associated with each number (as indicated in the code at the top of the page). In a second condition, the relationship between the digits and symbols was reversed. The patients were presented with four rows of symbols and had to copy the digit associated with the symbol. Figure 6.1 shows the various digit-symbol (standard) and symbol-digit (reversed) pairings used in the study.

The major rationale for using the reversed digit-symbol and the nonverbal symbols was to increase the perceptual demands of the task. The reversed digit-symbol condition required more perceptual search of the symbols than did the standard format of presentation. In the standard format, the subject had simply to locate a familiar digit (e.g., 2) in an ordered sequence (1–9), and then copy the symbol associated with the indicated digit. However, in the reversed format the subject had to search a series of unrelated and unordered symbols to locate a single symbol and the digit associated with it. The verbal-

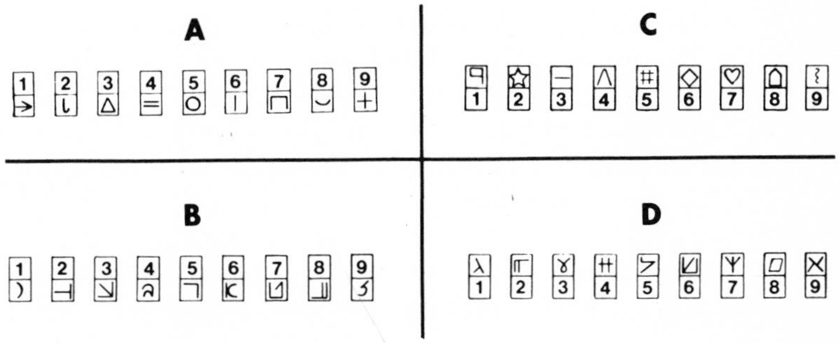

FIGURE 6.1 *Illustrated here are the stimulus items for the digit-symbol (A,B) and symbol-digit (C,D) pairings.*

TABLE 6.1

Mean Processing Time (sec) on Substitution Tests

Group	Symbol substitution (standard administration)		Digit substitution (reversed administration)	
	Familiar symbols	Unfamiliar symbols	Familiar symbols	Unfamiliar symbols
Normal	1.086	1.351	1.324	1.685
Alcoholic	1.365	1.455	1.693	2.392
Alcoholic Korsakoff	1.789	1.993	2.296	3.847
Right-hemispheric brain damage	3.251	3.078	5.432	6.762

izability or familiarity of the symbols further complicated the perceptual processes needed to perform these tasks, as the more verbalizable and familiar the symbol, the more quickly the subject could analyze and process the symbol. It was felt that if the alcoholic Korsakoff patients, like RBD patients, were impaired in their visuo-perceptive capacities, then both of these groups should be more affected by the digit-symbol modifications than should normal individuals.

The results of this study are shown in Table 6.1. The measure employed—substitution or processing time (sec)—is corrected for differences in the speed with which subjects could copy digits and the two types of symbols. Therefore, the measure reflects the amount of time needed to process a single digit-symbol or symbol-digit pair. Although reversing the task and using unfamiliar symbols did produce small, but significant, increments in the processing time of the normal group, these procedures had far greater effects on the processing times of the three patient populations. Alcoholic Korsakoff patients and RBD patients were most affected by the perceptual demands of the task, but the alcoholic control group was also significantly retarded in their processing of the materials.

Glosser *et al.* (1977) also correlated performance on the digit-symbol tasks with performance on a verbal, paired-associate learning test and on a children's visual embedded-figure test (Witkin, Oltman, Raskin, & Karp, 1971). Substitution time on the digit-symbol tasks did not correlate ($r = -.08$) with correct responses on the paired-associate task, but there was a significant correlation ($r = -0.57$)

between performances on the embedded figures test and processing times on the digit-symbol tasks. Consequently, although alcoholic Korsakoff patients were severely impaired on both the embedded figures and verbal paired-associate tasks, only their performance on the embedded figures test appeared to be related to their digit-symbol performance. It seems, then, that the alcoholic Korsakoff patients, like the RBD patients, have some visuoperceptive defect impairing their performance on the digit-symbol and probably other, perceptual memory tasks. It should also be noted that, as in the Glosser *et al.* (1976) study, the chronic alcoholic group showed cognitive defects that paralleled the impairments of the alcoholic Korsakoff patients. Although their perceptual deficits are not as severe as those of the alcoholic Korsakoff group, the patterns of impairment are qualitatively similar. Perhaps the processing deficits of the alcoholic Korsakoff patients do not develop acutely and may be found in subdued form in chronic, non-Korsakoff alcoholic patients. This issue will be discussed more fully in Chapter 10.

Although the Glosser *et al.* (1977) investigation demonstrated that the alcoholic Korsakoff patients' impairment on digit-symbol substitution tasks involved some higher order perceptual capacity, the exact nature of this visuoperceptive deficit was not determined. Kapur and Butters (1977), building upon the Glosser *et al.* (1977) results, assessed the role of visual scanning, learning, and contour analysis in the alcoholic Korsakoff patients' visuoperceptive problems on the digit-symbol task. As the digit-symbol task requires a systematic search of a visual stimulus, the oculomotor impairments associated with the Wernicke-Korsakoff syndrome (Victor *et al.,* 1971) might be expected to limit the patients' ability to scan an array of stimuli in an appropriate manner. Alternatively, because the digit-symbol task may involve a learning component, poor digit-symbol performance might reflect a failure to learn the location of a particular digit or symbol, or difficulty in remembering which symbols are associated with particular digits. Additionally, a deficit in analyzing the contours of geometric symbols may be a third factor involved. The previously noted (Glosser *et al.,* 1977) association between performance on digit-symbol and embedded figures tests makes this third factor a primary suspect.

Eleven alcoholic Korsakoff patients, 12 long-term alcoholics, and 11 normal individuals were administered the digit-symbol subtest from the WAIS, a symbol-digit, paired-associate learning task, a test of visual location learning, a visual search task, and an embedded figures test.

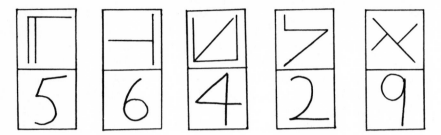

FIGURE 6.2 *The drawings illustrate the symbol-digit, paired-associate learning task items.*

On the symbol-digit, paired-associate test, the subjects were asked to associate five, unfamiliar geometric patterns with single-digit numbers, so that when they were shown a particular geometric pattern they could supply the associated digit. Figure 6.2 shows the five symbol-digit pairings. Ten learning and test trials were administered to each subject.

The visual search test consisted of 32 stimulus arrays, one of which is shown in Figure 6.3. Each array consisted of a target figure located in the center of the card and nine "search" figures in a horizontal line at the top of the card. On 16 of the 32 cards, the target stimulus was repeated among the search stimuli. The stimulus cards were presented tachistoscopically and were exposed until the subject indicated, by saying "yes" or "no" into a voice key, whether the target was repeated among the nine search stimuli. The appearance of a stimulus card in the tachistoscope triggered a timer which stopped when the voice key was activated.

The embedded figures task involved the presentation of 20 arrays of embedded figures such as the one shown in Figure 6.4. Each array consisted of a single, simple geometric figure that was embedded in one of four complex figures shown below the simple figure. The arrays

FIGURE 6.3 *This illustration is an example of visual-search test item card.*

FIGURE 6.4 *This illustration is an example of embedded-figures test items.*

were presented tachistoscopically and remained in view until the subjects indicated which of the four complex patterns contained the sample figure.

On the location learning task, the patients had to learn to associate a single-digit number and vertical black marker with a specific location along the horizontal axis of a 15- × 10-cm white card. Five cards were used, each with a different number and location for the vertical marker. On each trial, the subjects were given a blank card and a number and then asked to draw a vertical marker in the exact location associated with that number. Immediate feedback as to the correctness of the response was always given. All subjects were tested for 10 test trials.

The results indicated that, although group differences did not reach statistical significance for the visual search test, both the alcoholic Korsakoff and chronic alcoholic groups performed more poorly than did the normal control group on the other four tests. Table 6.2 shows the mean scores on the WAIS digit-symbol, embedded figures, and visual search tests, and Figures 6.5 and 6.6 present the results for the visual-location learning test and the symbol-digit, paired-associate task, respectively. It is evident from this table and the figures that the alcoholic Korsakoff and alcoholic groups were severely impaired.

The patients' scores on the digit-symbol test were correlated with

TABLE 6.2

Mean Scores on Digit–Symbol, Embedded Figures, and Visual Search Tests

Group	Digit–symbol	Embedded figures	Visual search (speed in sec)	
			Left	Right
Normal control	47.91	16.91	2.216	2.121
Alcoholic	36.08	11.33	2.758	2.826
Alcoholic Korsakoff	30.9	11.82	2.663	2.686

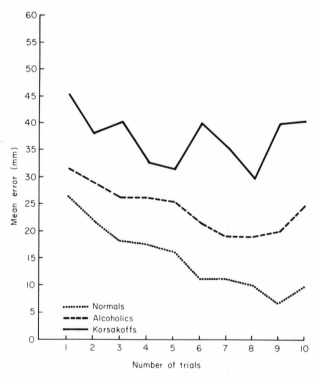

FIGURE 6.5 *The graph illustrates the mean error length during the visual-location learning test of normal control, long-term alcoholic, and alcoholic Korsakoff patients.*

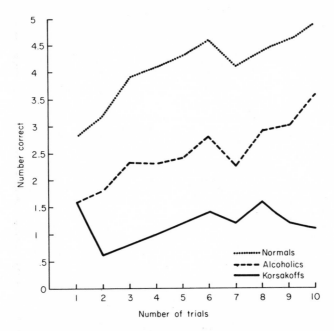

FIGURE 6.6 *The graph illustrates the mean number of correct responses on the symbol-digit, paired-associate learning test for normal control, alcoholic, and alcoholic Korsakoff patients.*

their scores on the remaining four tests, with separate computations for each of the three groups. The normal controls showed a significant correlation between symbol-digit, paired-associate learning and WAIS digit-symbol performance $(r = .71)$. The alcoholic Korsakoff patients displayed a significant correlation between scores on embedded figures and the WAIS digit-symbol test $(r = .68)$. For the chronic (non-Korsakoff) alcoholics, WAIS digit-symbol performance correlated with both symbol-digit learning $(r = .61)$ and embedded figures $(r = .73)$. None of the other correlations approached significance.

This differential pattern of deficits and intragroup correlations points to some of the factors contributing to the alcoholic Korsakoff and control groups' digit-symbol performances. Normal subjects' performance on the digit-symbol test is determined largely by their ability to learn the digit-symbol code. Once a given digit-symbol pairing is acquired, there is no need to refer to the code at the top of the test sheet. The more quickly the code is learned, the more items an individual will complete in the 90-sec test period. Compared with controls, all alcoholic Korsakoff patients are severely impaired in their ability to acquire new information (including digit-symbol and symbol-digit pairings), and, therefore, must employ a piecemeal perceptual strategy on this substitution task. Rather than rely on learned digit-symbol associations to facilitate performance, the alcoholic Korsakoff patients are limited to locating and analyzing each of the symbols to be copied. As shown by their poor scores on the embedded figures test, these patients are impaired in such visual contour analysis, and their degree of deficit acts as a good predictor of their digit-symbol scores. It appears then that the severe visuoperceptive deficits of alcoholic Korsakoff patients on the WAIS digit-symbol test are related to a combination of two problems: their well-known incapacity to learn new associations and a problem in contour analysis.

The findings of the Glosser *et al.* (1977) and the Kapur and Butters (1977) studies confirm the presence of visuoperceptive difficulties in non-Korsakoff alcoholics, and are consistent with the notion that some continuity exists in the perceptual deficits of alcoholic Korsakoff patients and long-term alcoholics. Although the difficulties the alcoholics encountered with the WAIS digit-symbol and the embedded figures tasks have been reported previously (for review, see Goodwin & Hill, 1975; Kleinknecht & Goldstein, 1972), impairments in the perceptual learning of detoxified alcoholics have not been routinely demonstrated (Butters, Cermak, Montgomery, & Adinolfi, 1977; Parsons & Prigatano, 1977). On the first recall trial of the symbol-digit association task, the alcoholics without Korsakoff's syndrome were as severely impaired as the Korsakoff patients. Although these long-term alcoholics evidenced some learning during the 10 test trials, their performance remained consistently inferior to that of the control group's. Even the intragroup correlations suggested that these alcoholics occupied a position (on some scale of deficit) midway between those of the control group and the alcoholic Korsakoff patients: The digit-symbol performance of these alcoholics correlated significantly with symbol-digit associative learning (as was the case with the control group) and the embedded figures task (as was the case with the alcoholic Korsakoff patients). In view of the present findings and recent pneumoencephalographic and brain scan demonstrations of cortical and subcortical atrophy in long-term alcoholics (e.g., Brewer & Perrett, 1971; Fox, Ramsey, Huckman, & Proske, 1976), it seems possible that the perceptual deficits of alcoholic Korsakoff patients and alcoholics may be attributable to involvement of similar brain structures (see Chapter 10 for further discussion).

LIMITED ENCODING AND THE ALCOHOLIC KORSAKOFF PATIENT'S DEFICITS IN FACE PERCEPTION

It is evident from the studies reviewed in this chapter that alcoholic Korsakoff patients demonstrate deficits on perceptual tasks that require extensive analyses of complex stimuli. One may ask whether this visuoperceptive deficit is yet another example of their general limitation in stimulus analysis. Visual stimuli, like verbal materials, are often multi-dimensional, and a limited or deficient analysis of these dimensions might result in a degraded percept, concept, and eventually engram that is later difficult to retrieve. We have seen, in previous chapters, that there is much evidence that alcoholic Korsakoff patients do not analyze all the characteristics of verbal materials (i.e., they evidence a failure in encoding), and we shall now review some recent evidence that a similar processing deficiency might play some role in their visuoperceptual problems.

Oscar-Berman and Samuels (1977) trained alcoholic Korsakoff patients to discriminate between complex visual stimuli differing in a number of relevant dimensions (e.g., color, form, size, position) and then administered transfer tasks to determine which of the relevant stimulus dimensions had been noted. While the intact controls showed transfer for all of the relevant stimulus dimensions, the alcoholic Korsakoff patients' discriminations were based on only one or two relevant features (e.g., color, size) of the stimuli. Oscar-Berman and Samuels believe that this incomplete analysis of stimulus dimensions may be responsible for the alcoholic Korsakoff patients' perseverative tendencies (i.e., inability to shift sets or cognitive strategies) on concept formation tasks (Oscar-Berman, 1973).

To further assess the possibility that the alcoholic Korsakoff patients' visuoperceptive problems might be attributable to a deficiency in the extent of their nonverbal analysis, Dricker, Butters, Berman, Samuels, and Carey (1978) employed a series of facial, recognition and matching tasks. These facial tests were chosen because recognition of unfamiliar faces appears to be a nonverbal task depending upon the integrity of the right hemisphere (Benton & Van Allen, 1968; DeRenzi & Spinnler, 1966; Milner, 1968), and because methods have recently been developed for assessing the attributes an individual uses in recognizing and matching unfamiliar faces. One test, developed by Carey and Diamond (1977), compares the use of paraphernalia, expression, and configurational facial cues. They found that 6- and 8-year-old children rely heavily upon superficial paraphernalia to determine identity of unfamiliar faces, whereas older children (e.g., 10 years) shift to the adult strategy of analyzing the complex configurational relationships (e.g., the spatial relationships between the nose, mouth, and eyes). The young child, but not the adult, will judge two photographs of faces to be identical when both models are wearing the same hat or have the same hair style. It was felt that if alcoholic Korsakoff patients tend to analyze only the superficial characteristics of patterned visual stimuli, then their performance on the Carey–Diamond facial recognition task should be qualitatively similar to that of children.

Three sets of facial recognition and matching tests were administered to 13 alcoholic Korsakoff patients, 8 RBD patients, 13 long-term alcoholics, and 14 normal individuals. On the first test, the subjects were presented with two sets of photographs of college students. Set 1 was a 4×3 array of 12 photographs. The subjects were allowed to inspect the array for 45 sec, after which the photographs were removed. After 90 sec, the subjects were given a 5×5 matrix of 25 photographs and asked to select the 12 faces that had appeared in the original inspection set. The second test was similar to the first, but only required that the subjects match (rather than recognize) faces. The subjects were presented, simultaneously, with a 5×5 matrix of photographs, a single (target) photograph of a face, and then asked to find the target face among the 25 comparison photographs. If the subject selected an incorrect face, he was told to continue looking until he found the correct match. This matching procedure was repeated for 12 individual target photographs.

The third test, developed by Carey and Diamond (1977), compares the subjects' tendency to use superficial piecemeal cues (such as paraphernalia and expression) and more advanced configurational cues in their analyses of faces. (The term "configurational relationships" refers to the spatial relationships between the nose, mouth, and eyes.) As shown in Figure 6.7, this matching test involves five basic problems. On each trial of a given problem, the subject is shown a card with

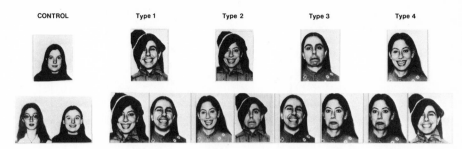

FIGURE 6.7 *Illustrated here are examples of control and problem items from the Diamond-Carey Faces Test. Types 1 and 2 contain paraphernalia to mislead subjects whereas types 3 and 4 use expression.*

three photographs of unfamiliar faces, one at the top (the target face) and two at the bottom (the comparison faces). The subject is asked to indicate which of the two comparison faces is the same as the one at the top of the card. In Type 1 and 2 problems, paraphernalia (e.g, a hat) is used to fool the subjects; if the subject bases identity on similar paraphernalia he has made an incorrect choice. In Type 3 and 4 problems, expression is used to fool the subject and judgments based upon similar expressions (smiling or frowning) would be incorrect. To perform consistently well on these four problem types, the subject must rely on the configurational aspects of the faces. In addition to the four experimental problems, there was a control problem in which neither paraphernalia nor expression were manipulated to fool the subjects. To qualify for inclusion in this study, a patient had to demonstrate accurate performance on the control problems.

The results from the first two tests are shown in Figure 6.8. On both tests, the alcoholic Korsakoff patients and the RBD patients were severely impaired. In fact, the performances of these two patient groups on the delayed identification test were not significantly better than chance. This deficit cannot be attributed simply to a memory problem, because both patient groups encountered some difficulty with the immediate identification (simultaneous matching from sample) task. It appeared, then, that the alcoholic Korsakoff and RBD patients have some deficit in the way they perceptually analyze the features of unfamiliar faces.

The nature of this encoding deficit becomes clearer when one examines the results of the Carey–Diamond matching task (Figure 6.9). The alcoholic Korsakoff and the RBD patients were often fooled by

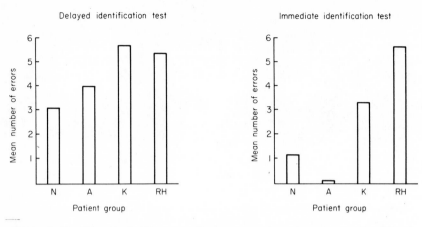

FIGURE 6.8 *The graph illustrates the mean number of errors on the delayed and immediate face identification tests (N = normal control group, A = alcoholics, K = alcoholic Korsakoff patients, RH = patients with right hemisphere damage).*

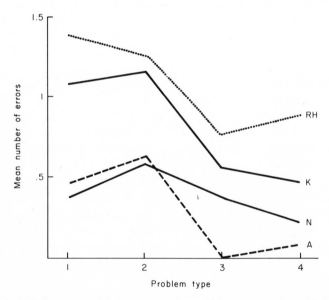

FIGURE 6.9 *The graph illustrates the mean number of errors on the Diamond-Carey Faces Test, problem Types 1–4 (N = normal controls, A = alcoholics, K = alcoholic Korsakoff patients, RH = patients with right hemisphere damage).*

both paraphernalia and expression in their matching of faces, although paraphernalia seems to be the more distracting of the two cues. These findings suggest that alcoholic Korsakoff patients (as well as RBD patients) might not analyze all of the relevant features of unfamiliar faces. Although normal subjects utilize the configurational features of faces, the alcoholic Korsakoff patients seem to rely upon more piecemeal or superficial features, such as paraphernalia and expression, and seem to ignore the configurational features of faces. If such limited perceptual analysis is characteristic of these patients, it may at least partially explain their difficulties in learning, remembering, and even perceiving nonverbal patterned materials. Just as the amnesics may fail to retrieve verbal materials because of faulty or incomplete analysis, so a similar impairment in perceptual processing may be responsible for the patients' nonverbal visual memory and perceptual deficits.

What is the neurological basis for the similarities in the behavioral deficits of the alcoholic Korsakoff and the RBD patients? Similarities were noted not only in this study of face perception by Dricker *et al.* (1978), but also in the digit-symbol study by Glosser *et al.* (1977). At least two explanations seem equally plausible.

1. Deficits in perceptual encoding may follow either cortical (RBD patients) or subcortical (Korsakoff patients) lesions. For the alcoholic Korsakoff patients, this deficit in perceptual encoding is only a single examplar of a general deficiency in the extent of the patients' verbal and nonverbal information processing, whereas for the RBD patients, the encoding problem may be limited to the visual modality. Jarho's (1973) report that traumatic injury to diencephalic structures results in both amnesic and visuoperceptive problems is consistent with this explanation.

2. The alcoholic Korsakoff patients' impairment in perceptual analysis may reflect some general cortical atrophy, in addition to their well-known subcortical diencephalic lesions (Victor *et al.,* 1971). The numerous neurological studies (Brewer & Perrett, 1971; Epstein, Pisani, & Fawcett, 1977; Fox *et al.,* 1976) linking atrophy of the frontal and parietal lobes to long-term alcoholism support this interpretation. Two other papers (Samuels, Butters, Goodglass, & Brody, 1971; Samuels, Butters, & Goodglass, 1971), dealing specifically with comparisons of the memory deficits of alcoholic Korsakoff patients and patients with RBD, have found that the two groups have very

109

similar forgetting curves for visually presented geometric patterns, with one qualitative exception. The forgetting of the patients with RBD was limited almost exclusively to material presented in the left visual field, whereas the alcoholic Korsakoff patients showed no such field specificity in their forgetting. The alcoholic Korsakoff patients were equally impaired in their retention of materials exposed to their left and right visual fields.

Despite this qualitative difference, the results of the present studies leave little doubt that alcoholic Korsakoff patients are impaired in their processing of nonverbal as well as verbal information, and that a limited encoding hypothesis remains a viable explanation of their cognitive problems.

Some mention should also be made of the unimpaired performance of the long-term (non-Korsakoff) alcoholics on the faces tests used by Dricker *et al.* (1978). A number of our studies (Butters *et al.,* 1977; Glosser *et al.,* 1977; Kapur & Butters, 1977) and those of other investigators (Goldstein, 1976; Goodwin & Hill, 1975; Parsons, 1975; Parsons, Tarter, & Jones, 1971) have reported that chronic alcoholics manifest visuoperceptive deficits similar to those of alcoholic Korsakoff and RBD patients. Therefore, one might have anticipated that the alcoholics would show some impairments on the facial recognition and matching tasks. This apparent discrepancy in the continuity between long-term alcoholics and the alcoholic Korsakoff and RBD groups may be rooted in the alcoholics' degree of brain damage and the complexity of the various testing instruments. As the alcoholics' cortical and subcortical atrophy is probably less extensive than the brain damage of alcoholic Korsakoff and RBD patients, their behavioral deficits may be apparent only on the most complex visuoperceptive tasks. The facial recognition and matching tasks may have been too easy to tap the alcoholics' minimal organicity.

7

Alternative Theories Of Amnesia

The theory of amnesia that has been developed throughout the course of this book, and described most specifically in Chapter 5, is only one of many advanced. Several other theories have proven to be quite valuable as frameworks for the development of logical series of experiments. Some theories have attempted to explain all forms of amnesia regardless of etiology, whereas others have dealt with a limited number of patients with a specific etiology. In most of these latter cases, including that of our own theory, these theories have proven to be more descriptive, rather than explanatory, of the amnesic syndrome. This limitation leaves much to be desired, but after all, if the amnesic syndrome were completely understood, there would be no need for theorizing. Consequently, none of the theories should be considered final or complete, but rather should be viewed as frameworks within which to conduct research.

CONSOLIDATION

The oldest theory of amnesia emerged from the work of Hebb (1949), who has been credited with developing one of the first modern neurological models of memory. In his system Hebb proposed that the brain could retain information in one of two ways: first, through the continual reverberation of a neural circuit, and second, through an actual structural change in neural patterning. Memory based on reverberating circuitry was felt to be quite susceptible to the effects of decay, because once the continued reverberation (i.e., rehearsal) stopped, the pattern's representation would begin to fade. In order to form a more permanent memory a second change, which was felt to be structural,

111

had to take place. Because this structural change took time to develop, it had to depend, in part, on the continual activation of the neural circuit until the transformation could be completed. This transformation came to be known as *consolidation*.

Brenda Milner (1968) has been the major advocate of a consolidation deficit theory of amnesia. She has based her theoretical viewpoint largely on the evidence gleaned from patient H. M., who became amnesic following a bilateral temporal lobectomy for the treatment of intractible seizures. Milner has suggested that the amnesic can form something resembling Hebb's "reverberating traces," but lacks the ability to transform the trace into a permanent "structure." Thus, the patient can function in the immediate present, but can never establish any lasting memories of moments past. It is this very proposition that has been interpreted as meaning that amnesics have intact short-term memories (STM) in the presence of totally deficient long-term memories (LTM), and, if STM is defined in this rather limited manner, then the case is well founded. But, as we have seen, once other proposed characteristics of STM are examined, problems with this dichotomy begin to emerge. Consolidation theory, however, does not stand or fall on the basis of a particular definition of STM.

The clinical examination of an amnesic patient provides two pieces of evidence to support Milner's consolidation theory. One is the demonstration that most amnesics (including alcoholic Korsakoff patients) can retain material as long as they are permitted to rehearse, but forget the information as soon as rehearsal ceases. The second bit of evidence consists of Milner's observation, confirmed by Marslen-Wilson and Teuber's (1975) formal documentation, that H. M. can remember much of his life prior to surgery but few of his experiences following surgery. This separation of remote and new memories indicates that what was presurgically consolidated is still retrievable, but what has occurred since cannot be retrieved because it has never achieved a permanent (i.e., structural) status.

Other evidence for consolidation comes largely from studies either with animals or patients who are receiving electroconvulsive shock (ECS). In both cases it has been observed that when ECS occurs shortly after learning, memory of that learning is lost. The major difficulty with these studies has been the estimation of the maximum length of time between learning and ECS that produces the amnesic condition. Although everyone agrees that the length of this interval can be taken as representing the length of time needed to consolidate the memory trace, no agreement on its duration has ever been achieved. Chorover and Schiller (1965) have estimated this interval in terms of seconds; Pearlman, Sharpless, and Jarvick (1961) have proposed that it takes several days; and Flexner, Flexner, and Stellar (1963) found evidence that consolidation can be disrupted several weeks after learning. Thus, the process of consolidation has never been linked to a specific time frame, and, in some cases, it has been found to continue long after reverberation must have ceased.

Quite apart from these difficulties in providing a converging operation for consolidation, the theory has not proven to be especially fruitful as a full explanation of amnesia. As mentioned above, the theory is a descriptive one in that it states the well-documented fact that only continually recirculated (i.e., rehearsed) material can be retained by amnesics. Beyond this, consolidation theory really adds nothing to our understanding of the amnesic's inability to retain material after short periods of distraction. Also, as Baddeley (1975) points out, consolidation theory is extremely hard pressed to explain why some forms of cueing (e.g., phonemic, semantic) can elicit memories or why the patients perform better on recognition versus recall tests. Why, for instance, can cueing elicit a correct response that, theoretically, was never consolidated? As we shall see, these problems are not restricted solely to the consolidation deficit theory.

RETRIEVAL-INTERFERENCE THEORY

The retrieval-interference theory proposed by Warrington and Weiskrantz (1970, 1973) has been a major model of amnesia. According to this viewpoint, amnesic patients encode and store information in normal fashion but are unable to retrieve specific material from LTM because of interference. Although amnesics may utilize normal retrieval strategies, they seem to be highly sensitive to interference from competing information and to have great difficulty in inhibiting this irrelevant material. This theory proposes that items in LTM are poorly insulated from one another and are in constant competition during the retrieval process. Thus, when alcoholic Korsakoff or other amnesic patients are asked the name of their physician for the fifth or sixth time, they continue to provide an incorrect answer because they cannot differentiate the physician's name from all the other names they have stored in LTM.

Warrington and Weiskrantz (1970, 1973) have provided two forms of support for their retrieval-interference theory: the presence of prior-item intrusions, and the beneficial effect of partial information at the time of retrieval. Prior-item (or prior-list) intrusions are evident when an amnesic patient is asked to learn two or more lists of words successively. For example, if List A is not too long, the amnesic patient may recall most of the items, but on List B and each succeeding list, the patient's performance becomes progressively worse in comparison to his retention of List A. Both Weiskrantz and Warrington (1970b) and Baddeley and Warrington (1970) have drawn attention to the fact that the large number of wrong responses (e.g., on List B) represent intrusions from previous lists (e.g., from List A). It appears that once words from List A attain LTM, they interfere with the patient's attempts to retrieve words from List B. A similar intrusion effect has been noted during paired-associate learning (Winocur & Weiskrantz, 1976). If patients attempt to learn two successive lists of verbal paired-associates that share the same stimulus but different response elements (e.g., List A = shop—rose; List B = shop—tray), their performance on List B will be marked by few correct associations and many intrusions from List A.

Further evidence for the retrieval-interference theory has emanated from procedures that manipulate the cues available at the time of retrieval. Warrington and Weiskrantz (1970) presented amnesic patients and control subjects with a short list of words. After a 1-min delay period, they tested retention with one of four procedures: free recall, yes-no recognition, cueing with the first three letters of each word, or cueing with a fragmented form of each word. The results are shown in Table 7.1. An analysis of variance performed on this data showed a significant interaction between groups and the method of testing. Although the amnesic patients were severely impaired when recall and recognition procedures were used, there were no significant group differences with the two "partial information" methods (i.e., initial letters, fragmented words). As the amnesics performed best with partial information techniques and the controls performed best with the recognition procedure, the investigators concluded that there was a differential effect of testing conditions in the two groups. The partial information methods facilitated the retrieval of the amnesic patients because the initial letters (and fragmented words) limited the number of items that could interfere with the patients' attempts to retrieve the previously presented words. Because normal controls

TABLE 7.1
Retention Scores after 1 Min [a]

	Controls $(N = 8)$	Amnesics $(N = 4)$
Recall	13.0	8.0
Recognition	18.7	10.5
Fragmented words	11.1	11.5
Initial letters	16.0	14.5

[a] From Warrington & Weiskrantz, 1970. Reproduced by permission.

were not as sensitive to interference as the amnesic patients, their retention was not facilitated by the limitations placed upon interference.

Despite the elegance of the retrieval-interference theory, a number of investigators (including Warrington and Weiskrantz themselves) have noted empirical and theoretical difficulties with this approach. Woods and Piercy (1974) questioned whether the partial information phenomenon was peculiar to amnesics, or whether it also characterized normal memory when traces were weak or inadequately stored. Normal subjects were presented with lists of words and tested for retention of half the material 1 min later, and the other half of the material 1 week after presentation. One group of subjects was tested with the yes–no recognition procedure, one with initial letters, and one with fragmented words. The major finding of this study was that the differences between the 1-min and 1-week retentions paralleled the differences between the normals and amnesics reported by Warrington and Weiskrantz (1970). A significant interaction was found between delay interval and method of testing. Although yes–no recognition was significantly poorer after the 1-week versus the 1-min delay interval, the partial information techniques did not yield significantly different performances with the two delay intervals. It appears, then, that if an intact individual's memories are weakened by the passage of time, their retrieval can also be facilitated by the use of partial information. This finding questions whether Warrington and Weiskrantz' partial information experiments have uncovered any special processing problems of amnesic patients. As Piercy (1977) has noted, "It may be incautious to say more than that, when tested after one minute, the differential effect of test conditions on amnesic memory

115

is more like that of normals tested after one week than of normals tested after one minute. Such a statement does not of course provide support for any particular hypothesis concerning the nature of the amnesic defect [p. 40]."

Woods and Piercy (1974) and Piercy (1977) have also questioned evidence based upon prior-list intrusions. In their experiments, normal subjects evidenced a high incidence of false-positive responses when initial letters served as the partial information. In fact, the incidence of false positives was higher with initial letters than with the yes–no recognition procedure. If intrusion errors are an indicator of sensitivity to interference, they should *not* have been most prevalent with test conditions that facilitated retention. Given the overall retention differences between the yes–no recognition and partial information procedures, one would have expected the incidence of false-positive responses to be higher for the recognition procedure. Similarly, when Piercy (1977) recalculated Baddeley and Warrington's (1970) data to determine the *proportion of total errors* (rather than the proportion of total responses) that were prior-list intrusions, the results did not support retrieval-interference theory. Of the amnesics' wrong responses, 45% were prior-list intrusions, whereas 69% of the normal subjects' errors were this type. If the amnesics' difficulties in retaining List B items were due to interference from List A items, then the amnesics, not the control group, should have had the higher percentage of intrusion errors.

Warrington and Weiskrantz (1978) have also reported a series of experiments that necessitate modification of their original retrieval-interference theory. In the main experiment of this series, the effect of prior-list learning on the learning of a second list was evaluated. High proactive interference was assured by the use of word pairs that were the only two words having the first three letters in common. For instance, the word "cyclone" appeared on one list, and the word "cycle" on the other list. Each word on List 1 was presented once visually, and retention was tested immediately by presenting the first three letters of each word on the list (i.e., cued recall). Immediately following this test of List 1 retention, List 2 was shown to the subjects and a cued retention test of the second list followed without delay. In all, four presentation and cued retention trials of List 2 were administered. The results indicated that although the amnesic patients performed more poorly overall than did the normal control group, this difference became progressively greater as the testing proceeded. On

List 1 retention and the first retention trial for List 2, no significant differences were noted between the two groups: Both groups performed more poorly on the first retention trial of List 2 than on the single List 1 retention trial, but this decrement was equal for both groups. The differences between the amnesics and normal subjects appeared on the second, third, and fourth retention trials of List 2, and the differences increased with each succeeding retention trial.

As the investigators note, List 1 words were expected to interfere with the learning of words on List 2, but the effect of this proactive interference should have been greater for the amnesic patients than for the normal subjects. Also, interference theory predicts that differences between amnesic and normal individuals should have been greatest on the first retention trial of List 2 and should have decreased with each successive presentation of List 2. As the results of this experiment are the opposite of those predicted, Warrington and Weiskrantz seem justified in concluding that the amnesics' retrieval difficulties cannot be accounted for by a simple interference model.

Another problem for retrieval-interference theory is its inability to account for much of the published data on retrograde amnesia. A detailed review of the recent literature on retrograde amnesia was presented in Chapter 1, so only brief mention of the central issues pertaining to the problem will be discussed at this time. If retrieval theory is to be accepted in its present form, then amnesic patients should manifest retrograde amnesias of equal severity for all periods of their lives. It should be as difficult to retrieve names and events from the 1930s as from the 1960s. Any increased sensitivity to interference, both proactive and retroactive, should be as detrimental for the retrieval of events learned 20 years ago as for events acquired 5 years ago. However, the majority of published investigations do not show this "flat" retrograde amnesia. Clinical and experimental studies of retrograde amnesia (e.g., Albert *et al.,* 1979a; Marslen-Wilson & Teuber, 1975; Seltzer & Benson, 1974) have all demonstrated the existence of a temporal gradient in which there is a relative sparing of the alcoholic Korsakoff patients' most remote memories. Although Sanders and Warrington (1971) have argued persuasively that many tests of retrograde amnesia have included easier questions about the remote versus the recent past, Albert *et al.* (1979a) have found temporal gradients with tests that statistically control for item difficulty. Furthermore, Squire and his colleagues (Squire, 1975; Squire, Slater, & Chace, 1975) have studied the retrograde amnesia of depressed patients

117

receiving electroconvulsive therapy (ECT). These investigations employed questionnaires about public events and TV programs that were famous or were aired for very limited periods of time. Even with this stringent control for exposure and item difficulty, the patients receiving ECT revealed retrograde amnesias with the classical temporal gradient. They had a significant loss of memory for events and programs that had occurred during the past year, while their memory remained intact for events that were newsworthy several years before ECT was begun. It is not clear how a theory of amnesia based solely on retrieval mechanisms could account for these results.

These recent experiments should not be taken as evidence that interference and retrieval problems do not exist for alcoholic Korsakoff patients. On the contrary, our own investigations of high and low proactive interference (Chapter 4) support the conclusion that patients with Korsakoff's syndrome have dramatic problems in this area. The point we are attempting to emphasize is that increased sensitivity to interference may not be a sufficient explanation of their retrieval and general memory impairments. The possibility exists that these increases in sensitivity to interference are a reflection of an incomplete, or partial, encoding of stimulus materials. Retention based on partially analyzed, verbal, and nonverbal stimuli may be more sensitive to interference than retention of fully analyzed materials. If such is the case, then the apparent retrieval and interference problems of amnesic patients, in general, may be secondary to a defect in the analysis of information at the time of storage. It is not unreasonable to assume that poorly stored information will be difficult to retrieve at a later time, despite the presence of intact retrieval strategies.

CONTEXTUAL THEORY

Several recently presented theories of the amnesic syndrome have emphasized the alcoholic Korsakoff patients' inability to discriminate context (see, for example, Kinsbourne & Wood, 1975; or Winocur & Kinsbourne, 1976, 1978). It has been proposed that amnesics are unable to discriminate the context in which something is learned and, consequently, are easily confused between recently presented "experimental" material and information acquired in the distant past. Sanders and Warrington (1971) also invoke this possibility as an attempt to explain confabulation that occurred during their retrograde amnesia experiment. They described it as a sort of "early experience being reported out of context." Basically, contextual theory can be summarized as follows: The amnesic has a nearly normal acquisition and storage ability except for his failure to discriminate between the spatial and temporal "contextual cues" associated with different experiences (Winocur & Kinsbourne, 1976, 1978). As a result of this deficit, the patient cannot retrieve specific information because the context in which it was learned cannot be reconstructed.

Evidence supporting this theory of a "disorder in contextual discrimination" can be found in an experiment by Huppert and Piercy (1976). These investigators showed 80 pictures to each subject (alcoholic Korsakoff and control) on Day 1, and then 80 more on Day 2. Day 2 pictures consisted of 40 new pictures and 40 repeats from Day 1. Ten minutes after the exposure of the eightieth picture on Day 2, the subject was presented with 160 pictures and asked to respond both to the question, "Did you ever see this picture before?" and to the question "Was it presented today?" Of the 160 pictures 120 had been exposed previously (on Day 1 and/or Day 2), and 40 were "fillers" that had not been used on either day. The alcoholic Korsakoff patients had no trouble with the first question, but demonstrated many false positives in answering the second question. In other words, the patients frequently said they had seen pictures on Day 2 that had actually been presented *only* on Day 1. It seemed that context had been lost, even though the specific information remained. Repeated pictures and Day-2-only pictures were recognized quite well by these patients: Once a picture was seen it was retained, but the context in which it had been viewed was lost.

Kinsbourne and Wood (1975) emphasize the patients' inability to discriminate context to explain their observation that alcoholic Korsakoff patients have impaired episodic memory. They note that Tulving (1972) defined semantic memory as being relatively independent of the context in which it was learned, whereas episodic memory is totally dependent upon contextual retention. Thus, Kinsbourne and Wood argue that the alcoholic Korsakoff patients' episodic memory is impaired because contextual retention is impaired. They further speculate that the patients' semantic memory is normal because context does not play a role in this type of retention. Although this latter assumption does not necessarily follow from the evidence on contextual forgetting, the Kinsbourne and Wood theory does provide an additional explanation for forgetting from episodic memory.

Winocur and Weiskrantz (1976) found that alchololic Korsakoff patients could learn a list of paired-associates when the stimuli were in some way related to the responses, but could not learn a subsequent list which employed the same stimulus elements as the first. They interpreted this result as meaning that the patients were unable to inhibit List 1 responses because of their inability to separate the context of List 1 from that of List 2. However, their task did not provide a real test of this proposal, so in a related experiment, Winocur and Kinsbourne (1976) sought to demonstrate that the greater the discriminability between the context of List 1 and List 2 learning, the greater the probability that alcoholic Korsakoff patients would be able to learn and remember List 2. They accomplished this discriminability by printing the stimulus materials from List 1 and List 2 on different colored cards, reducing the intrusion errors on List 2 from 70% to 38%. (Interestingly, though, this procedure did not increase the learning rate significantly.) In another procedure, they translated each stimulus from List 1 to List 2 by combining the List 1 stimulus and response and using this combination as the stimulus in List 2. For example, "battle–soldier" in List 1 became "battle, soldier–army" in List 2. They felt that this manipulation would eliminate interference by circumventing any tendency to emit the List 1 response during List 2 learning. It turned out to be a successful ploy, but, unfortunately, one cannot determine conclusively that the patients were aware of the relationship between List 1 and List 2 stimuli. Finally, Winocur and Kinsbourne (1978) reported two additional methods for increasing the saliency of the contextual cues for the alcoholic Korsakoff patients. Introducing a 3-min walk between the learning of the two lists and changing the room illumination for each list were measures sufficient to reduce interference from List 1 during the alcoholic Korsakoff patients' attempts to learn List 2.

Although context theory does seem to have more explanatory value than consolidation or interference models, it does have two very serious shortcomings. First, although it is often proposed as a retrieval deficit theory, it might be more easily viewed as an encoding deficit theory. If it is simply hypothesized that context is one of many stimulus attributes that can be analyzed, then one can propose that contextual forgetting is just one more case of faulty analysis by these patients. Huppert and Piercy's data might be interpreted as indicating that context was never part of the patients' analysis during Day 1 presentation, and Winocur and Kinsbourne's paired-associate data might be similarly handled. Indeed, their "brief-walk" data are more easily explained by assuming a context-encoding deficit, rather than a context-retrieval problem. The second problem is that context has not proven to be a very robust cue for normal subjects under most conditions of retrieval. For this reason, it seems peculiar to explain *all* of the alcoholic Korsakoff patients' forgetting as being due to the loss of this one, rather minor, cue. Under some experimental conditions, it can be made robust, and perhaps under these conditions it does explain episodic impairments of these patients. But under conditions where semantic cues are emphasized, memory based on this cue also suffers.

OTHER THEORETICAL APPROACHES

There exist two other theories of amnesia that are casually mentioned from time to time. However, these theories have not been as fully articulated as those that have just been presented. In one case, the theory has been forwarded simply to explain one small set of data, and in the other case, the theory has been extrapolated from the animal literature.

Imagery Deficit

Baddeley (1975) proposes that if one accepts Paivio's (1971) division of verbal episodic memory into linguistic and imaginal systems, then it may follow that amnesics are impaired in their ability to use the imaginal features of verbal information, while not necessarily being impaired in the linguistic. His evidence comes from a study in which amnesics profited, on a retention task, from word clustering based on taxonomic categories, but did not find clustering by visual imagery to be a useful technique. Cermak (1975) has also found that the generation of imagery is difficult for these patients. However, he noted that when the patients are cued for the image at retrieval, this procedure proved to be at least as useful as semantic cues. Thus, Baddeley's suggestion that the imaginal aspect of verbal analysis is impaired in alcoholic Korsakoff patients may be true, but such an impairment is not likely to underlie the patients' entire verbal memory deficit. In fact, it may provide yet another example of the faulty qualitative analysis done by these patients during the acquisition stage of information processing.

121

Cognitive Disorganization

O'Keefe and Nadel (1978) have proposed a theory of human amnesia based upon investigations with hippocampectomized animals. These authors reported that animals with hippocampal lesions can learn responses to stimuli, but are unable to develop a cognitive map of an area or maze that would allow them to demonstrate awareness of the environment and locate food on the basis of cues. Extrapolating from these results, O'Keefe and Nadel hypothesize that verbal learning may involve the formation of a "semantic" map, and that the ability to form such cognitive structures may depend upon the integrity of the limbic system. It may be too early to judge this model, as little evidence currently exists to support or refute it. However, it appears that if the esoteric phraseology of "cognitive maps" is taken away, one is left with a semantic encoding deficit model.

THEORETICAL CONCLUSIONS

One problem inherent within any theory is the tendency to view the theory as being an end-product based entirely upon the research that preceded it. Pragmatically speaking, however, theories generally serve best as frameworks for the generation of new research, and a theory's value in the long run might best be determined by the stimulating effect it has on productive research. If the theories described in this chapter are judged in this manner, their value can be readily seen. However, if each is judged purely by the amount of data it seems capable of encompassing, then each falls short of total applicability. None of the theories is complete, primarily because each has focused, a priori, on a favored aspect of the entire processing continuum. This criticism is as true for the theory described in Chapter 5 as it is for those presented in this chapter. Some emphasize the encoding or registration aspect of information processing, some the storage aspect, and some the retrieval portion. Unfortunately, as many theorists of normal memory have begun to realize, these "stages" of processing are so highly interactive and interdependent that the impairment of one would always be reflected in the impairment of another. It is quite clear that these aspects of information processing are not separable in normal memory, so it is unreasonable, it would seem, to expect to be able to separate them neatly in the amnesic syndrome.

This assessment does not mean that the relative importance of one aspect of processing over another should not be studied, but rather that no one portion of the totality should be postulated as being "absolutely" responsible for a deficiency in overall memory. Just as normal memory theorists focus research on specific aspects of processing, amnesia researchers should continue to do so. However, this should not be done at the expense of denying the involvement of other aspects. It is entirely possible that registration, storage, and retrieval are all somewhat impaired in amnesia, and that both qualitative and quantitative deficits exist at each stage. This is tantamount to saying that deficits in memory should be thought of as being deficits in information processing, just as normal memory is now considered to be the result of normal information processing. In short, we must cease to quibble over absolute contributions suggested by our partial theories and work to see the relative contributions of each. We must also seek to determine whether these relative contributions are the same for all types of amnesics.

8

Are All Amnesics Alike?

So far, this book has focused on the neuropsychological features of a particular group of amnesic patients, namely, alcoholic Korsakoff patients. These patients have been characterized as exhibiting a specific constellation of information processing deficits evidenced by their performance on tests of short-term memory (STM), encoding, and perception. Germane to such neuropsychological investigations is the issue of the applicability of these findings to other groups of patients with severe memory disorders. It could be asked whether the severe memory problems of alcoholic Korsakoff patients, patients with progressive dementias, and patients who have survived encephalitis all involve the same information processing deficits, or whether these different etiologies result in distinctive patterns of cognitive impairments. Because amnesia has been associated with a number of etiologies (e.g., vascular, alcoholic, viral, traumatic) and brain sites (e.g., hippocampus, mammillary bodies, midline thalamus), it is of some importance to determine whether all amnesias reflect the same underlying impairments.

Warrington and her collaborators have proposed that amnesia is a unitary disorder regardless of the etiology or locus of the disease (e.g., Baddeley & Warrington, 1970; Warrington & Weiskrantz, 1973). Their amnesic population has included patients with alcoholic, viral, anoxic, and surgical etiologies, and they have reported that all patients perform similarly on their various learning and cognitive tasks. Normal STM, increased sensitivity to proactive interference, and flat retrograde amnesias exist similarly in all their amnesics, regardless of etiology. However, studies from our own laboratory and reports from some other investigators suggest that there may be differences among the memory disorders of various amnesic and dementing populations. The present chapter will review some of these differences.

MEMORY DISORDERS OF POSTENCEPHALITIC PATIENTS

When the herpes simplex virus attacks the brain (i.e., herpes encephalitis), the majority of patients die, remain in a vegetative state, or are left with a severe general dementia. However, a few postencephalitics survive and appear to have few intellectual deficits except for a severe amnesic disorder. The virus damages substantial portions of the anterior temporal lobe, including the hippocampus, amygdala, uncus, and surrounding neocortex. However, the patients' memory problems are usually attributed to atrophy of the hippocampus. Their major behavioral symptoms are similar to those of alcoholic Korsakoff patients and include both anterograde and retrograde amnesia. The neuropathology and clinical symptomatology of this disorder have been well described by Drachman and his associates (Drachman & Adams, 1962; Drachman & Arbit, 1966).

In view of the clinical similarities in the memory disorders of the alcoholic Korsakoff and postencephalitic patients, one might suspect that similar information processing deficits might be involved in the two disorders. To assess this possibility, Lhermitte and Signoret (1972) compared the performance of alcoholic Korsakoff and postencephalitic patients on four memory tasks. Their tests involved the learning and retention of a spatial array, a verbal sequence, a logical arrangement, and a code. On the first task, the alcoholic Korsakoff patients actually showed better retention than the postencephalitic patients. However, on the remaining three memory tests, the postencephalitics were not only superior to the Korsakoff patients, but did not differ significantly from a normal control group. From these results, Lhermitte and Signoret concluded that the memory disorders manifested by amnesics with different etiologies are probably not identical.

Lhermitte and Signoret's empirical differentiation of the alcohol- and virus-related amnesias has also received some support from our own investigations. Several memory and information-processing tests used with the alcoholic Korsakoff patients have now been administered to four patients who survived attacks of herpes simplex encephalitis. Figure 8.1 shows the performance of the four postencephalitics (V.J.,

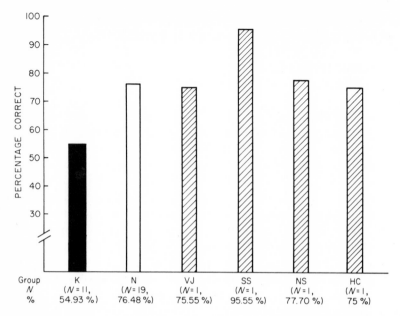

FIGURE 8.1 *The graph illustrates the performance of 4 postencephalitic (V.J., S.S., N.S., H.C.) patients, 11 alcoholic Korsakoff patients, and 19 normal controls on Peterson short-term memory task with consonant trigrams as the stimulus material. Reprinted with permission from* Empirical Studies of Alcoholism, *Copyright 1976, Ballinger Publishing Company.*

S.S., N.S., H.C.), 11 alcoholic Korsakoff patients, and 19 normal subjects on a Peterson short-term memory task in which consonant trigrams were the to-be-remembered stimuli. Although the alcoholic Korsakoff patients' performance is significantly impaired in comparison to the control group and the postencephalitic patients on this test, the recall of the postencephalitic subjects does not differ from that of the normal control group. In fact, one postencephalitic patient, S.S., had the highest recall score on the Peterson task. The patient, S.S., has been described in detail (Cermak, 1976), but for our present purpose it is important to point out that his anterograde and retrograde amnesias are so severe that he is still unable return to his position as an optical engineer.

Despite the postencephalitic patients' superiority on tests of STM, their performances on tests of retrograde amnesia are often worse than those of alcoholic Korsakoff patients and do not demonstrate the same temporal gradient discussed in Chapter 1. Figure 8.2 shows the performance of 11 alcoholic Korsakoff, 15 normal control, and 3

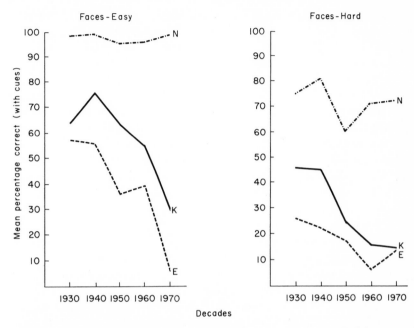

FIGURE 8.2 *The graph illustrates the performance of postencephalitic (E) and alcoholic Korsakoff (K) patients and normal controls (N) on* easy *and* hard *items of the Albert* et al. *Famous Faces Test.*

postencephalitic subjects on the Albert *et al.* (1979) famous faces test. For easy items, the encephalitic patients perform more poorly than the alcoholic Korsakoff patients. For hard items, the postencephalitic patients not only perform more poorly than the alcoholic Korsakoff patients, but also demonstrate only a slight temporal gradient in their retrograde problems. Additionally, items from the remote past are as difficult to recall as faces from the recent past for the postencephalitic group. It may be of some interest that postencephalitic, but not the alcoholic Korsakoff, patients provide data consistent with Sanders and Warrington's (1971) conceptions of retrograde amnesia.

Conclusions based on these findings should be made cautiously as, of the four encephalitis patients, only S.S. and H.C. are still truly amnesic upon clinical examination. At present, V.J. still has memory impairments that interfere with her daily life, but she has returned to work as a secretary and cannot be considered amnesic by the usual clinical criteria. Although N.S. was amnesic at the time the STM tests were administered, she has made a full recovery since and now displays neither anterograde nor retrograde memory problems. Furthermore, all four encephalitis patients differ from the average Korsakoff patient in educational attainment, IQ, socioeconomic class, and, perhaps, in other factors that may contribute to their normal performance on the STM task.

Despite these cautions, some speculations concerning the double dissociation between the alcoholic Korsakoff and encephalitic patients on the STM and retrograde amnesia tasks are in order. This dissociation not only emphasizes possible differences among amnesic populations, but also suggests that anterograde and retrograde amnesic symptoms may not necessarily be correlated (Benson & Geschwind, 1967). The ability to retain new information and the capacity to recall past events may depend on different cognitive processes and, ultimately, on different neuroanatomical structures. Certainly, Fedio and Van Buren's (1974) demonstration that anterograde and retrograde deficits may be separated by stimulation along the anterior–posterior axis of the left temporal lobe is consistent with the noted behavioral dissociations. The subjects for their study were patients with left, or right, focal epileptogenic lesions who were being considered for unilateral, anterior temporal lobectomy to relieve intractable seizures. Neuropsychological testing was conducted while the patients received intracranial stimulation to determine the location of language areas within their temporal lobes. The results showed that stimulation of the anterior sectors of the left temporal lobe resulted in a failure to consolidate or store verbal materials presented simultaneously with the stimulation (i.e., anterograde amnesia). In contrast, stimulation of the posterior sectors of the temporal lobe resulted in an inability to recall verbal material that had been presented shortly before the onset of stimulation (i.e., retrograde amnesia).

INDIVIDUAL CASE STUDIES

Although generalizations from individual cases must always be made with extreme caution, intensive investigation of an unusual or rare patient can often supply important clues that lead eventually to a new direction for systematic research, and ultimately to new discoveries about brain–behavior relationships. Dr. Brenda Milner's patient, H.M., falls into this category of case study, and we shall dwell upon those features of this patient's disorder that are relevant to the theme of this chapter. Some reference will also be made to a patient (N.A.) whose amnesia was studied by Teuber (Teuber, Milner, & Vaughan, 1968) and more recently by Squire (Squire & Moore, 1979; Squire & Slater, 1978). Comparisons of H.M. and N.A. with our population of alcoholic Korsakoff patients emphasize the diversity of anterograde and retrograde symptoms that can be manifested by amnesic patients.

Scoville and Milner (1957) described the severe memory disorder of a young man who had undergone bilateral, mesial, temporal lobe ablations to treat an uncontrolled form of epilepsy. Although H.M.'s surgery was successful as far as saving his life, he was left with a severe and permanent anterograde amnesia that has been extensively studied by Milner, her colleagues, and students (for reviews, see Milner, 1966, 1970). Following surgery, H.M. had trouble learning his new address and the names of new acquaintances, and he had difficulty recalling events that had occurred a few hours previously. He was able to learn and retain simple motor skills like the pursuit rotor task (Corkin, 1968), but he was unable to master a 28-choice point tactile maze after 215 trials. When Milner, Corkin, and Teuber (1968) subsequently tested H.M. on a shorter version (7 choice points) of the maze, he was still impaired but did attain the learning criterion after 155 trials. However, and most remarkable, when H.M. was tested on this short maze 2 years later, he showed 75% savings, despite the fact that he did not remember being tested on the task previously. Apparently, although H.M. has great difficulty in learning new materials, once information does achieve the status of long-term storage, it can be retained fairly well.

H.M. has been reported to have severe STM disorders. Prisko (1963) assessed H.M.'s STM deficit by employing a modification of the Konorski matching-from-sample technique. In this procedure, the patient is presented with two stimuli from the same modality that are separated by delay intervals ranging from 0 to 60 sec. The patient is then asked to indicate whether the second stimulus was identical to, or different from, the first. Prisko employed nonverbal visual stimuli (light flashes, shades of red, nonsense figures) and auditory stimuli (clicks, tones). Although normal subjects rarely made errors on this task, H.M.'s performance deteriorated markedly with longer delays. Sidman, Stoddard, and Mohr (1968) confirmed Prisko's findings by presenting a sample ellipse to H.M. and then, after a given delay period (ranging from 0 to 40 sec), asking him to choose the identical ellipse from among eight ellipses. Although H.M. performed normally when there was no delay on this test, he evidenced severe impairments in identifying the correct ellipse with delays greater than 5 sec.

This brief review underlines several similarities between H.M.'s major symptoms and those of alcoholic Korsakoff patients. H.M. and the alcoholic Korsakoff patients have difficulty learning new information, are impaired on tests of STM, can learn simple motor tasks, and can retain materials to some extent once that information has attained long-term storage. There are, however, two major differences to be noted. One is that there are significant differences in the retrograde amnesias of H.M. and the alcoholic Korsakoff patients. The alcoholic Korsakoff patients' inability to recall past events involves at least the two decades immediately prior to the onset of their illness whereas, H.M.'s retrograde deficits are more limited. H.M. cannot recall events that occurred during the 2–3 years prior to his operation, but events before this 3-year period are recalled normally.

H.M.'s limited retrograde deficit is somewhat perplexing when one considers the very severe, retrograde memory problems of postencephalitic patients. Because the memory problems of both H.M. and postencephalitic patients have been attributed to bilateral destruction of the hippocampi within the mesial temporal region, one might anticipate that their memory disorders would be quantitatively and qualitatively similar. One possible explanation for this difference may involve the extent of hippocampal and temporal lobe damage. If Fedio and Van Buren (1974) are correct about the separation of anterograde and retrograde problems along the anterior–posterior axis of the temporal lobe, then it is possible that the postencephalitic patients have more extensive (and posterior) temporal lobe damage than H.M. The fact that postencephalitics often have mild aphasic disorders certainly suggests that their lesions extend more posteriorly and laterally than H.M.'s anterior and mesial surgical ablation. Presumably, the more posterior the lesion, the more severe the patient's retrograde amnesia would be.

This separation of anterograde and retrograde memory deficits has also been reported for the extensively studied, amnesic patient, N.A. (Squire & Moore, 1979; Squire & Slater, 1978; Teuber, Milner, & Vaughan, 1968). This male patient was 22-years old at the time he was injured in 1960 when a fencing foil entered his right nostril and punctured the base of his brain. This injury apparently produced a stable lesion localized in the left dorsal medial thalamus adjacent to the third ventricle (Squire & Moore, 1979). Although his I.Q. remains intact, N.A. has a severe impairment in learning new verbal materials. This verbal anterograde amnesia is evident not only upon clinical examination, but also with numerous experimental paradigms such as paired-associate learning, Peterson STM tasks, and continuous recognition tests (i.e., identification of recurring words). Despite the severity of this anterograde amnesia, N.A. has little difficulty recalling events prior to his accident. Squire and Slater (1978) have assessed his remote memory with recall and recognition tests that included questions about public events and television programs from the 1950s, 1960s and 1970s. As anticipated on the basis of his severe verbal anterograde amnesia, N.A. was unable to recall public events and TV programs that had occurred or been broadcast since his injury in 1960. However, for the 10 years prior to his injury (1950–1959), N.A.'s recall of public events and television programs was normal!

The second major difference between H.M. and alcoholic Korsakoff patients concerns their rate of forgetting. Huppert and Piercy (1977, 1978) have reported that when normal control groups, H.M., and alcoholic Korsakoff patients attain the same level of learning, important differences emerge in their rates of forgetting over a 7-day period. They showed each patient 120 slides of colored pictures photographed from magazines. The subjects' recognition memory for these pictures was tested 10 min, 1 day, and 7 days later. During each recognition test, 40 of the original (i.e., previously exposed) slides and 40 new (i.e., not previously exposed) slides were presented in a random order, and the subject was asked to indicate with a yes or no response whether he had seen each slide before. To insure that all subjects would attain approximately the same level of learning at the 10-min delay period, exposure time during the initial presentation of the slides was manipulated to insure a performance level of 75% correct. For the normal control group, each slide had to be exposed for only 1 sec to attain this 75% level after a 10-min delay; for the amnesic patients, exposure times of 4 to 8 sec were necessary to attain this level of correct recognition. Thus, an increased rehearsal time led to a significant improvement in the learning of the amnesic patients.

The results of Huppert and Piercy's study demonstrated that recognition performance declined with increasing retention intervals (1 day, 7 days) for the control group, alcoholic Korsakoff patients, and H.M. However, the rate of decline did not differ for the normal control group and alcoholic Korsakoff patients over this 7-day period, whereas H.M.'s performance revealed a much steeper rate of forgetting than the other two groups. Huppert and Piercy conclude, on the basis of their results, that the anterograde amnesias of H.M. and the alcoholic Korsakoff patients involve different deficits in information processing. The alcoholic Korsakoff patients' difficulties may emanate from a lack of stimulus analysis or encoding. When provided with sufficient time to fully analyze a complex stimulus, these patients are capable of learning, and demonstrate normal recognition memory over an extended period of time. H.M.'s rapid decline in recognition cannot, however, be accounted for by such a cognitive deficit. Huppert and Piercy suggest that H.M.'s difficulty in learning new material may also reflect a deficit in stimulus analysis, but that his inability to retain newly learned material may be an indicator of an additional problem with consolidation and storage.

COMPARISONS OF ALCOHOLIC KORSAKOFF AND DEMENTING PATIENTS

Severe memory disorders are not unique to amnesic patients. In fact, complaints about memory (anterograde and retrograde) are among the first symptoms of progressive dementing disorders (Miller, 1977). The major difference between pure amnesia and progressive dementias is that the memory loss of the dementing patient is part of a general intellectual decline. Although the amnesic patient's IQ usually remains within the normal range despite his severely impaired memory quotient, the IQ and the memory quotient of the dementing patient progressively decline as the illness advances. IQ and memory quotient scores in the 80s are common relatively early in the dementing process. Given our concern with cognitive factors in memory, there is a critical question as to whether the severe memory disorders displayed by dementing and amnesic patients reflect the same deficits in information processing. Do concepts like increased sensitivity to proactive interference (PI) and failures in encoding and stimulus analysis help us to understand the dementing patients' difficulty in acquiring new information?

Three recent studies (Butters & Grady, 1977; Butters, Tarlow, Cermak, and Sax, 1976; Meudell, Butters, & Montgomery, 1978) comparing the memory disorders of alcoholic Korsakoff patients and of patients with Huntington's Disease (HD) provide some evidence that

132

different cognitive deficits are involved in the patients' anterograde memory disorders. Patients with Huntington's Disease have a genetically transmitted disorder that results in a progressive atrophy of the basal ganglia and cerebral cortex. Their most common behavioral symptoms include involuntary choretic movements and a progressive dementia, with severe memory problems forming part of the general intellectual decline (Caine, Ebert, & Weingartner, 1977).

On STM tests, HD patients perform as poorly as do the alcoholic Korsakoff patients (Butters *et al.*, 1976). Figure 8.3 shows the performance of alcoholic control, alcoholic Korsakoff, and HD patients on a Peterson distractor task with consonant trigrams as the to-be-

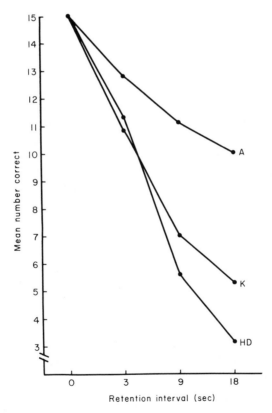

FIGURE 8.3 *The graph illustrates the performance of patients with Huntington's Disease (HD), alcoholic controls (A), and alcoholic Korsakoff patients (K) on a Peterson short-term memory test with consonant trigrams as the stimulus material.*

remembered material. Similar results have been reported for word triads and single words (Butters *et al.*, 1976; Butters & Grady, 1977; Meudell *et al.*, 1978).

Despite the similarity in the STM scores, an analysis of the types of errors made by the two patient groups indicates that distinctive processes may underlie their impaired performances. Meudell *et al.* (1978) distinguished three types of errors (omission errors, prior-item intrusions, extra-list intrusions) that would be made on a distractor task when word triads are used as the stimulus material. An *omission error* was defined as a failure to respond with any words (e.g., "I can't remember the words"). A *prior-item intrusion* was defined as a response with a word(s) that had been presented on a previous trial. For example, if "fish" was one of the to-be-remembered words on Trial 1 but continued to be given as an answer on Trials 2 and 3, the patient was credited with two, prior-item intrusion errors. Errors labeled *extra-list intrusions* were responses that were not among the stimulus words comprising the test. Although the HD and alcoholic Korsakoff patients make approximately the same number of total errors on this STM task (Figure 8.4), the two groups can be differentiated according to the types of errors they produced. The alcoholic Korsakoff patients made many prior-item intrusions, but the HD

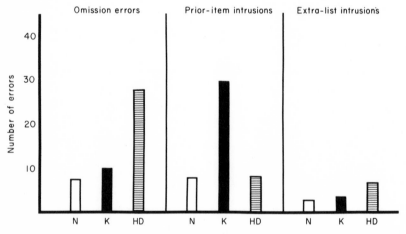

FIGURE 8.4 *The graph illustrates the types of errors made by patients with Huntington's Disease (HD), normal control (N), and alcoholic Korsakoff patients (K) on Peterson short-term memory test with word triads as the stimulus material.*

patients made primarily omission errors. Neither patient group produced many extra-list intrusions.

This differentiation of the two groups provides some hints as to the
nature of their STM impairments. The alcoholic Korsakoff patients'
intrusion errors are consistent with previously reviewed evidence of
their sensitivity to PI. An item remembered on Trial 1 (e.g., "fish")
may interfere with the patient's attempts to retain new material on
Trials 2 and 3. The lack of prior-item intrusions for the HD patients
suggests that interference may not be an important factor in their
impaired STM performances. This interpretation is supported by two
other experiments in which the amount of PI in the test situation was
manipulated (Butters *et al.*, 1976). Figure 8.5 shows the results of a
study in which STM (with the Peterson technique) was evaluated
under massed (high PI) and distributed (low PI) presentation conditions. During massed presentation, a 6-sec rest interval was inter-

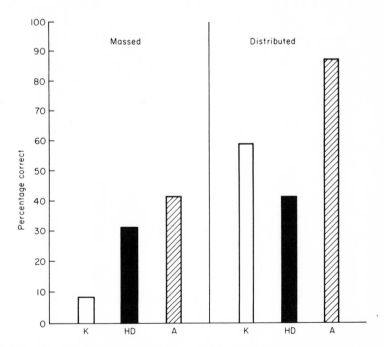

FIGURE 8.5 *The graph illustrates the mean percentage of correct under massed
and distributed presentation by patients with Huntington's Disease (HD), alcoholic
control (A), and alcoholic Korsakoff patients (K).*

spersed between trials. During distributed presentation, a 1-min rest interval was allowed between trials. With massed presentation, the HD patients recalled more items than the alcoholic Korsakoff patients; but with distributed presentations, the alcoholic Korsakoff patients did significantly better than the HD patients. The alcoholic Korsakoff patients and the alcoholic control group, but not the HD patients, were aided by the reduction in PI with distributed practice.

An identical outcome occurred in a second experiment that manipulated the amount of PI in the learning situation. The exact procedures followed in this experiment were described fully in Chapter 4. Briefly, the Peterson trials were divided into blocks of two with a 6-sec interval between trials. Then it was possible, simply by varying the similarity of the material presented on the two trials, to manipulate the amount of PI influencing the patient's recall on the second trial of each block. Figure 8.6 presents the results for the *second* trials of each block. As in the case of massed versus distributed practice,

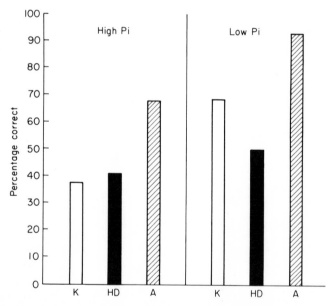

FIGURE 8.6 *The graph illustrates the mean percentage correct on high and low proactive interference (PI) conditions by patients with Huntington's Disease (HD), alcoholic control (A), and alcoholic Korsakoff patients (K). Reprinted with permission from* Empirical Studies of Alcoholism, *Copyright 1976, Ballinger Publishing Company.*

the alcoholic Korsakoff patients performed very poorly under high PI conditions (word triads on both trials) but improved significantly with conditions that minimized PI (consonant trigrams on the first trial, word triads on the second). The HD patients, however, did not demonstrate a similar improvement. Although the alcoholic Korsakoff and HD patients did not differ significantly under high PI conditions, the alcoholic Korsakoff patients recalled more words than the HD patients did under low PI conditions.

In addition to their differences in sensitivity to PI, the alcoholic Korsakoff and HD patients also performed differently on two encoding tasks (Butters et al., 1976). On a previously described task (Chapter 5) that compared free and cued (semantic cues) recall of eight-word lists, the alcoholic Korsakoff patients were impaired with cued, but not with free, recall. When this test was administered to HD patients, they were severely impaired regardless of the method of recall. The HD patients recalled significantly fewer words under both recall conditions than the alcoholic Korsakoff or alcoholic control groups.

The second encoding task was the false recognition test, also described in Chapter 5. On this test, the patients were instructed to note repetitions of words within a 60-word list. Some words were repeated, whereas other words were phonetically, associatively, or semantically related. The HD and alcoholic Korsakoff patients made different types of errors on this task. The alcoholic Korsakoff patients made significantly more false-positive errors (identifying a word as a repeat when it had not been presented previously) than the HD patients and control group; but the HD patients made more false-negative errors (failure to identify an actual repetition) than the other two groups.

Alcoholic Korsakoff and HD patients also differ in the degree to which they benefit from rehearsal. Butters and Grady (1977) employed a modified STM task (Peterson distractor technique) in which a 0-, 2-, or 4-sec delay intervened between the presentation of the to-be-recalled word triads and the beginning of the distractor (i.e., counting backward) procedure. The 2- and 4-sec predistractor delays were used to allow the patients additional time to rehearse the verbal stimuli. The results, shown in Figure 8.7, indicate that although the predistractor delays led to improved recall for the alcoholic Korsakoff patients, this experimental manipulation had virtually no effect on the recall of the HD patients. Therefore, it appeared that the alcoholic Korsakoff, but not the dementing HD, patients, were able to utilize

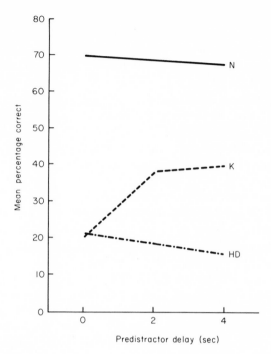

FIGURE 8.7 *The graph illustrates the performance of patients with Huntington's Disease (HD), normal control (N), and alcoholic Korsakoff patients (K), on Peterson short-term memory task with 0-, 2-, or 4-sec predistractor delays.*

the 2- and 4-sec predistractor delays to continue analysis of the stimulus features.

Most of our studies have focused on the alcoholic Korsakoff and HD patients' impairments in learning new materials. However, these patient groups can also be distinguished by their ability to recall remote events. Numerous studies (Albert *et al.*, 1979; Marslen-Wilson & Teuber, 1975; Seltzer & Benson, 1974) have demonstrated that the retrograde amnesia of alcoholic Korsakoff patients is characterized by a steep gradient with a differential sparing of memories from the 1930s and 1940s. On the other hand, when the Albert *et al.* (1979) retrograde amnesia battery was administered to 8 HD patients and 10 normal control individuals (Butters, Albert, & Sax, 1979), the results of the famous faces test and the recall and recognition questionnaires showed no evidence of a temporal gradient (Figure 8.8). Like the alcoholic Korsakoff patients, the HD patients are impaired in their

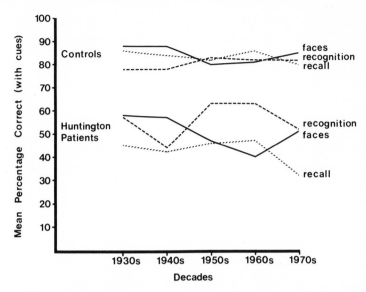

FIGURE 8.8   *The graph illustrates the performance of normal controls and patients with Huntington's Disease on the Famous Faces Test and the recall and recognition questionnaires from the Albert* et al. *retrograde amnesia battery.*

ability to identify and recall famous people and events, but their retrograde amnesia is flat and not characterized by a temporal gradient in which famous events and people from the 1930s and 1940s are differentially spared. The HD patients have as much difficulty recalling events and people from the 1930s and 1940s as they have recalling people and events from the 1960s.

The results of these studies strongly suggest that the information-processing deficits that underlie the HD patients' memory problems are different from those involved in the impairments of the alcoholic Korsakoff patients. However, although it is clear that the alcoholic Korsakoff patients have problems in their analyses of stimulus materials, the specific nature of the HD patients' processing problems is not understood. The pattern of deficits in the HD group may reflect a very severe form of the encoding deficits characterizing the disorders of the alcoholic Korsakoff patients. It is also possible that HD patients simply cannot store new information (i.e., they may fail to consolidate new information). The HD patients' failure to improve their performance with low PI conditions (Butters *et al.* 1976) and with increased time for rehearsal (Butters & Grady, 1977) is consistent with

139

the notion that these patients may lack some of the neuroanatomical structures necessary for consolidating and storing new information.

In summary, the findings reviewed in this chapter, although fragmentary, do not support the theory of amnesia as a unitary disorder. Patients with clinically similar amnesias can be differentiated on the basis of their performance on STM and retrograde amnesia tasks. In addition, amnesic and dementing patients with quantitatively similar STM impairments appear to have qualitatively different patterns of deficits when information processing is tested. It seems reasonable, therefore, to postulate that the general patient population with amnesic symptoms may be failing to retain and retrieve information for a variety of reasons.

9

Sensory Capacities

The main concern of this book has been the information-processing impairments of alcoholic patients with Korsakoff's syndrome and the ways in which these deficits affect memory and perception. We have described a series of experiments suggesting that inadequate analyses of stimulus materials may be responsible, at least in part, for the alcoholic Korsakoff patients' severe anterograde amnesia. An underlying assumption of this interpretation is that these patients are capable of normal registration of stimulus inputs. However, if the patients have basic sensory impairments, then any memory or encoding deficiency may be a secondary phenomenon confounded by a degraded or partial stimulus input. For this reason, any analyses of the alcoholic Korsakoff patients' problems in terms of information-processing deficits must include a full description of their sensory capacities.

Although Talland (1965) did not formally assess the sensory capacities of his patients, he anecdotally reported that nine of his alcoholic Korsakoff patients "seemed to have no capacity for olfactory discrimination." The known neuropathology of the Wernicke-Korsakoff syndrome provides an even firmer basis for suspecting deficiencies in the patients' chemical (olfactory and gustatory) senses. The dorsal medial nucleus of the thalamus (DMN), damaged in all Wernicke-Korsakoff patients with a clinically confirmed memory deficit in the Victor *et al.* series (1971), and the ventral medial nucleus of the thalamus (VMN), damaged in 58% of these same patients, are thought to be the two thalamic relays for the olfactory system in mammals (MacLeod, 1971). In addition, the mammillary bodies (MB), damaged in all of the Victor *et al.* (1971) series of Wernicke-Korsakoff patients, may also be capable of receiving olfactory input via the pyriform cortex, the lateral entorhinal area, and the hippocampus. Neuroanatomical studies of primates and rats show how olfactory input may reach the thalamic DMN, the thalamic VMN, and the MB. The olfactory bulb projects to the pyriform cortex via the lateral olfactory tract, and the DMN and the VMN of the thalamus, in turn, receive projections from the pyriform cortex. The pathway to the MB involves projections from the pyriform cortex to the lateral entorhinal area, from the lateral entorhinal area to the hippocampus, and from the hippocampus to the MB.

Motivated by these neuropathological and neuroanatomical considerations, Jones and her collaborators have assessed, in a series of three studies, the alcoholic Korsakoff patients' visual, auditory, olfactory, and gustatory senses. In the first investigation, Jones, Moskowitz, and Butters (1975a) studied simple discrimination and memory of odors by 14 alcoholic Korsakoff patients, 14 chronic alcoholics, and 14 nonalcoholic control individuals. The olfactory test used 10 relatively unfamiliar odorants (i.e., food essences and chemical compounds) in a sniff-bottle technique. There were two bottles of each odorant and 20 pairs were used, each odorant matched once with itself and once with another odorant. For each pair, the subject judged whether the second odorant was the same or different from the first. The 20 pairs were presented once with a 0-sec and once with a 30-sec interval between the two members of each pair. The 0-sec condition was considered a test of discriminatory ability, whereas the 30-sec condition evaluated the patients' ability to retain olfactory stimuli. For both conditions, there was a 30-sec interpair interval separating each test trial. Table 9.1 lists the contents of the 20 bottles and gives the 20 test pairings used by Jones et al. (1975). Before the test, each subject was asked to sniff five common kitchen odorants (e.g., cloves, ground coffee beans, orange extracts), to state whether or not he could smell each, and finally to identify each odorant. This procedure was intended to provide an independent assessment of the subject's olfactory function.

The most striking result of this initial study was the discovery of the alcoholic Korsakoff patients' severe impairment in olfactory discrimination. On the preliminary test dealing with common kitchen odorants, these patients were severely impaired in both the detection and identification of the substances. On the principal test with 0- and 30-sec delays, the alcoholic Korsakoff patients did not perform significantly better than chance. As seen in Figure 9.1, they averaged almost nine total errors in both delay conditions, and their scores are

TABLE 9.1
Odorants Used [a]

Bottle number and contents	Approximation of odor	Test pairs
1. Butyl acetate	Nail-polish remover	6–16
2. Rosemary	Rosemary	8–15
3. Allspice	Allspice	10–2
4. Sage	Sage	4–1
5. 1-Decanol	Fatty, oily	3–9
6. Rosemary	Rosemary	18–17
7. Benzaldehyde	Almonds, cherries	7–9
8. Terpinyl acetate	Pungent	4–14
9. Allspice	Allspice	5–19
10. Butanol	Denatured alcohol	20–15
11. Black walnut	Black walnut	11–17
12. d-p Mentha-1, 8 diene	Fruity	1–18
13. Butanol	Denatured alcohol	8–13
14. Sage	Sage	12–20
15. Terpinyl acetate	Pungent	2–6
16. Benzaldehyde	Almonds, cherries	7–16
17. Black walnut	Black walnut	3–19
18. Butyl acetate	Nail-polish remover	10–13
19. 1-Decanol	Fatty, oily	11–12
20. d-p Mentha-1, 8 diene	Fruity	5–14

[a] From Jones, B. P., Moskowitz, H. R., & Butlers, N., Olefactory discrimination in alcoholic Korsakoff patients, *Neuropsychologia*, 1975, *13*, 173–179.

considerably inferior to those of the alcoholics and the nonalcoholic control group.

Table 9.2 shows the types of errors made by the subjects on the two delay conditions. A false-positive error was defined as incorrectly

TABLE 9.2
Mean Error Scores on Olfactory Discrimination Test [a]

Groups	0-sec delay		30-sec delay	
	False positive	False negative	False positive	False negative
Korsakoff patients	6.3	2.6	4.8	3.8
Alcoholic controls	4.0	1.6	3.6	2.6
Nonalcoholic controls	1.9	2.3	2.4	3.1

[a] See footnote in Table 9.1.

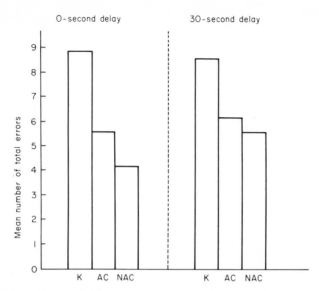

FIGURE 9.1 *The graph illustrates the mean number of total errors during olfactory testing at 0- and 30-sec delays. The groups represented are alcoholic Korsakoff patients (K), alcoholics (AC), and nonalcoholic control subjects (NAC).*

declaring two different odorants to be the same, and a false-negative error was defined as incorrectly declaring two identical odorants to be different. It is evident from this division of errors that the alcoholic Korsakoff patients made many more false-positive, but no more false-negative, errors than did the nonalcoholic control group. If the alcoholic Korsakoff patients are, as it appears, very impaired in olfactory discrimination, then it is reasonable to assume that different odors might tend to smell the same to them so that false-positive errors result. The alcoholics tended to show the same pattern of errors as the alcoholic Korsakoff patients, but the differences between the alcoholic and nonalcoholic groups were not statistically significant.

There are several possible explanations for the alcoholic Korsakoff patients' impaired discrimination of odor quality. One explanation is that the patients' threshold for the perception of olfactory stimuli might be elevated. These higher thresholds would result in poor odor detection and, ultimately, in impaired quality discriminations. A second explanation is that, although the threshold for odor perception remains normal, the alcoholic Korsakoff patients' ability to discriminate among odor qualities is selectively impaired. A third explanation is that the alcoholic Korsakoff patients might have a general cognitive deficit (e.g., an inability to make judgments involving two stimuli) that would result in impaired discriminations, regardless of the sensory modality tested. To test the first and third possibilities, Jones, Moskowitz, Butters, and Glosser (1975b) performed another experiment. Psychophysical methods of category scaling and magnitude estimation were used to assess the patients' judgments of visual, auditory, and olfactory stimuli. Such techniques allow both the measurement of sensory thresholds and a broad evaluation of the patients' perception of stimuli that are suprathreshold. It is possible for an individual to have normal intensity thresholds, yet still have an attenuated appreciation of moderately intense stimuli. Jones *et al.* (1975b) anticipated that the alcoholic patients with Korsakoff's syndrome would demonstrate deficits in their scaling of olfactory stimuli but show normal scaling of the visual and auditory stimuli.

Their second experiment included three groups of subjects: 10 alcoholic Korsakoff patients, 10 alcoholic control patients, and 10 nonalcoholic control individuals. Each subject was tested on scaling tasks involving assessment of stimulus intensity in vision (shades of gray), audition (loudness of noise), and olfactory (intensity of butanol odor). The procedures for testing all three modalities were the same. Two scaling methods were used for each modality: magnitude estimation (ME) and category scaling (CS). For CS, the patient was presented with a chart of numbers from 1 on the bottom to n on the top (n being the number of stimuli in the set for the particular modality being tested). After the examiner had presented both the weakest and the strongest stimulus once and had paired each with its appropriate number (i.e., 1 for the weakest, n for the strongest), the patient proceeded to the test stimuli. For each test stimulus, the patient indicated his perception of its intensity by pointing to an appropriate number on the chart.

In order to obtain MEs, the patients performed a line-matching task in which they indicated perceived intensity by adjusting the length of an unmarked, spring-loaded tape measure. The tape measure was embedded in one end of a block of wood and could be pulled out to any length. At the beginning of testing, a standard stimulus was chosen from the middle range of intensities and was matched with an intermediate extension of the tape measure. In one condition, the presentation of this standard occurred only once and that was at the beginning of a test session (ME 1). In a second condition, the standard

145

was presented before every test stimulus (ME 2). The patient was always instructed to pull the tape out to the length that best indicated the stimulus intensity. If the stimulus appeared more intense than the standard, the subject was to extend the tape further. If the test stimulus seemed weaker than the standard, he was to reduce the extension of the tape.

Eight Munsell neutral gray cards were used for assessment of the visual modality. The cards ranged from values 2–9 on the Munsell scale. (Value 2 was dark and value 9 very light.) For the auditory modality, six levels of white noise (ranging from 45 to 95 db) were presented binaurally to the patients via earphones. Olfactory judgments were assessed using six different saturation levels (ranging from .6% to 20% saturation) of N-butyl alcohol (butanol) that were presented to the patients with an air-dilution olfactometer.

The results of this experiment have been plotted in Figures 9.2, 9.3, and 9.4 in the form of intensity functions for all three modalities. The ME functions are plotted in log–log coordinates, whereas CS functions are plotted in semilog coordinates. In the visual modality (Figure 9.2), the functions for all three groups are superimposable for ME 1, ME 2, and for CS. The intensity functions for loudness (Figure 9.3) indicated that the alcoholic Korsakoff patients differed from the control groups on ME 1 by showing some recruitment or steepening. Even here, however, the function for the alcoholic Korsakoff patients intersects with that of the control groups. On ME 2 and CS, the alcoholic Korsakoff patients are indistinguishable from the two con-

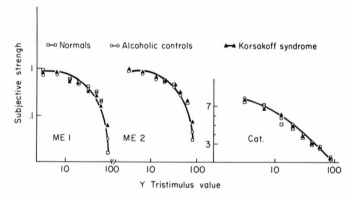

FIGURE 9.2 *The graph illustrates visual intensity functions derived from results of magnitude estimation (ME) and category-scaling (Cat.) tests.*

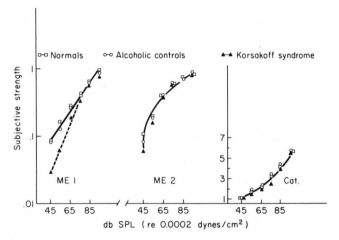

FIGURE 9.3 *The graph illustrates auditory intensity functions derived from results of magnitude estimation (ME) and category scaling (Cat.) tests.*

trol populations. Thus, on the basis of the auditory and visual functions, it appears that alcoholic Korsakoff patients can scale stimulus intensities in these modalities in a normal fashion.

The intensity functions for olfaction (Figure 9.4) indicate that the alcoholic Korsakoff patients are extremely impaired in their appreciation of the intensity of butanol. The ME and CS functions of this group differ markedly from those of the alcoholic and nonalcoholic control groups. The slope evidence for the MEs of the three lowest concentrations suggests that alcoholic Korsakoff patients do

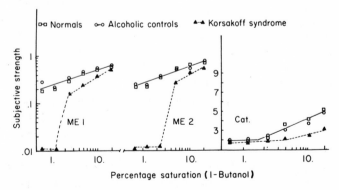

FIGURE 9.4 *The graph illustrates olfactory intensity functions derived from results of magnitude estimation (ME) and category-scaling (Cat.) tests.*

147

not, on the average, smell these levels of butanol. When olfactory threshold determinations were made, it was found that the Korsakoff group had the highest threshold value of the three groups of subjects.

The results of the second Jones et al. (1975) study indicate that the alcoholic Korsakoff patients' previously noted impairments in odor discriminations are, at least, partially related to elevated thresholds for the perception of odors. The steepening of the odor intensity function for the alcoholic Korsakoff patients parallels the steepening of the loudness function for patients with neural hearing losses, and suggests a neural olfactory deficit. It is also evident that alcoholic patients with Korsakoff's syndrome are not impaired in their psychophysical scaling of all sensory materials. In contrast with their severe problems in scaling olfactory intensities, they showed virtually no impairment in their scaling of visual and auditory stimuli. This latter finding does not support the hypothesis that the alcoholic Korsakoff patients' olfactory problems reflect a general cognitive impairment with all scaling and discrimination tasks.

In a third study, Jones, Butters, Moskowitz, and Montgomery (1978) attacked two issues that were unresolved by the first two studies. First, they asked whether alcoholic Wernicke-Korsakoff patients suffer an impairment of the other chemical sense, that of taste. The VMN of the thalamus, damaged in 58% of the Victor et al. (1971) series of Korsakoff patients, is thought to be the thalamic relay for the gustatory system (Burton & Benjamin, 1971). Although judgments of the stimulus quality of taste would obviously be impaired in a population already shown to have reduced olfactory sensitivity, judgments of the stimulus intensity of the four basic tastes are made independently of odor, and indeed, the strongest tasting substances, (e.g., sugars, salts, and many mineral acids) are often odorless. It seemed possible then that Wernicke-Korsakoff patients would have deficits in the scaling of taste intensities, but that their gustatory abnormality should be less striking than their olfactory impairment because a smaller percentage of these patients have the lesion postulated to result in a taste deficit.

Second, Jones had used only a single group of organic patients (i.e., the alcoholic Korsakoff group) in her first two studies, so some doubt remained concerning whether her reported olfactory deficits were specific to the alcoholic Korsakoff patients or represented a deficit manifested by all brain-damaged populations. That is, the olfactory scaling task might simply be more difficult than the visual or auditory ones, and thus could be the most sensitive to brain damage because of its complexity rather than its relationship to specific diencephalic nuclei. To control for such generalized effects of brain damage, Jones *et al.* (1978) now included a group of patients with right-hemispheric lesions. It has been well documented that patients with lesions of the nondominant right hemisphere are impaired on a variety of visual and visuospatial measures, such as the comprehension of cartoon drawings, the recognition of faces and nonsense figures, the visual organization of fragmented patterns, and the drawing of simple geometric forms (e.g., Milner, 1967; Warrington & James, 1967). Thus, in view of the severity of the visuoperceptual deficits of patients with right-hemispheric lesions, it was anticipated that these patients would be impaired in their scaling of visual materials (especially patterned ones), but would not show a deficit in their scaling of olfactory and gustatory stimuli.

Four groups of subjects were examined: 10 chronic alcoholics, 10 alcoholic Korsakoff patients, 10 patients with right-hemispheric damage, and 15 nonalcoholic normal control individuals. The groups were matched for age and did not contain individuals with histories of medical conditions associated with smell and taste disorders (e.g., viral hepatitis, Sjogren's syndrome, deviated septum). All of the patients having right-hemispheric damage were right-handed, and their lesions were verified on the basis of radiological investigation or surgical reports.

Each subject was tested on stimulus intensity assessment in each of six perceptual continua (olfactory, gustatory, auditory, and three visual continua). The nonpatterned visual continuum consisted of shades of gray, and the two patterned visual continua were circles of varying sizes and grids of varying complexity. The method of magnitude estimation (ME) was used, with subjects providing verbal responses (intensity estimates of 1–1000) to the stimuli. For each continuum, all stimuli for the task were presented in each of four consecutive randomized blocks, so that the subject judged each stimulus four times. Prior to each block of stimuli, a stimulus near the middle of the intensity range was demonstrated to the subject and matched with the number 200. This provided a standard of comparison for their subsequent judgments. The subjects were told to assign higher numbers to more intense stimuli and lower numbers to less intense stimuli.

The stimuli for the assessment of grayness were the same eight, Munsell neutral gray cards (Munsell values 2–9) as used in the previous

149

Jones *et al.* (1975) scaling experiment. The stimuli for the assessment of circle size were eight circles that were drawn in ink on white construction paper. The radii of the eight circles ranged from 5 to 134.2 mm. The third visual task was concerned with the complexity of contour and consisted of seven stimuli composed of a symmetrical arrangement of crossed lines within a 8-in. × 8-in. square. The index of complexity was the number of divisions in the grid, and the number of divisions ranged from 4 to 16,384.

In the auditory scaling task, seven levels of white noise, ranging from 35 to 95 db, were presented to the patients through earphones. Butanol again was the odorant used for olfactory scaling. It was administered through an eight-channel, air-dilution olfactometer. Eight intensity (i.e., saturation) levels, ranging from .16% to 20% saturation, were used. Eight different concentrations of sodium chloride in distilled water were used for the scaling of taste intensity. These concentrations ranged from .008 mole to 1.0 mole. The patient sipped about .25oz of solution from a small paper cup, held the solution in his mouth for a few seconds, and then expelled it before making a judgment. A distilled water rinse followed each test stimulus.

Three statistical analyses were performed on the patients' intensity ratings. One analysis involved the correlation coefficients between the patients' subjective intensity estimates and the objective stimulus intensities. If a patient group had a lower overall correlation coefficient on a particular scaling task than the control group, this decrement would indicate a more random, and therefore less accurate, scaling of the stimuli. The second statistical procedure was a two-way analysis of variance that was performed on the individuals' raw stimulus ratings (i.e., the mean of the four estimates) at each stimulus intensity level. In the case of the three sensory tasks, where a detection threshold estimate was feasible (e.g., audition, olfaction, gustation), a third analysis compared thresholds with a simple one-way analysis of variance.

The results of this experiment are best discussed on a group basis. The alcoholic Korsakoff patients showed their greatest deficits on the olfactory and gustatory scaling tasks. Figures 9.5 and 9.6 compare the intensity functions of the alcoholic Korsakoff patients and the normal control group on the olfactory and gustatory tasks, respectively. In both cases, the statistical analyses showed that the alcoholic Korsakoff patients rated the two strongest stimulus intensities as being weaker than the other groups did. The alcoholic Korsakoff patients also had

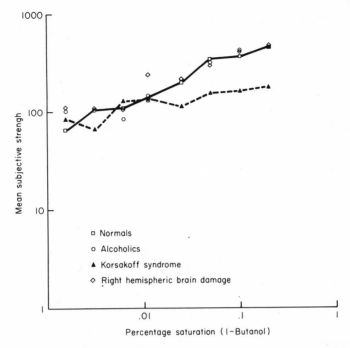

FIGURE 9.5 *The graph illustrates the group mean ratings of odor intensity, graphed on log–log coordinates.*

significantly lower, olfactory correlation coefficients (between stimulus intensity and subjective ratings) and higher olfactory thresholds than the other groups. For the taste task, however, the alcoholic Korsakoff patients' correlation coefficients and detection thresholds did not differ from the other groups.

In addition to their deficiencies in smell and taste, the alcoholic Korsakoff patients evidenced a slight problem with the scaling of the grids and circle sizes. Although the two-way analyses of variance of the stimulus ratings for these tasks revealed no significant differences between these patients and the normal control group, their correlation coefficients were significantly lower than those of the normal control group. There was no evidence of any differences between the alcoholic Korsakoff patients and normal control individuals on the scaling of grayness and sound intensities.

In striking contrast to the alcoholic Korsakoff patients, the patients with right-hemispheric damage were severely impaired in their scaling

151

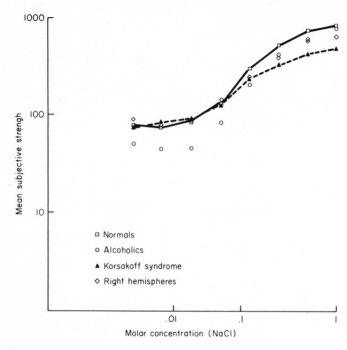

FIGURE 9.6 *The graph illustrates the group mean ratings of taste intensity, graphed on log–log coordinates.*

of all three visual stimuli, but had no difficulty in scaling olfactory and gustatory stimuli. Figures 9.7, 9.8, and 9.9 show the intensity functions of the patients with right-hemispheric damage and normal control individuals on the three visual tasks. The two-way analyses of variance for all three functions demonstrated significant differences between these brain-damaged patients and the other three groups. The two darkest shades of gray, the largest circle, and the two most complex grids were all rated significantly lower by the patients with right-hemispheric damage than by the other patient groups. The correlations between stimulus intensity and subjective ratings underscored the visual deficit of the right brain-damaged patients: For all three visual-scaling tasks, these patients had lower correlations than either the alcoholics or normal control individuals. The auditory scaling task failed to provide evidence of a consistent impairment in any of the patient groups, although the right brain-damaged patients tended to rate the loudest noise as being weaker than did the normal control subjects.

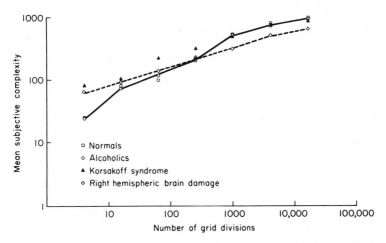

FIGURE 9.7 *The graph illustrates the group mean ratings of the complexity of various grids, graphed on log–log coordinates.*

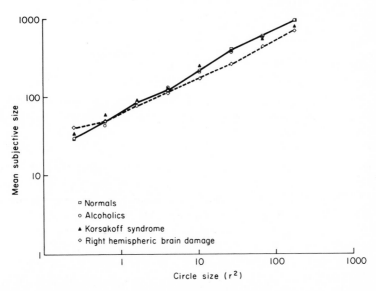

FIGURE 9.8 *The graph illustrates the group mean ratings of the size of differing circles, graphed on log–log coordinates.*

153

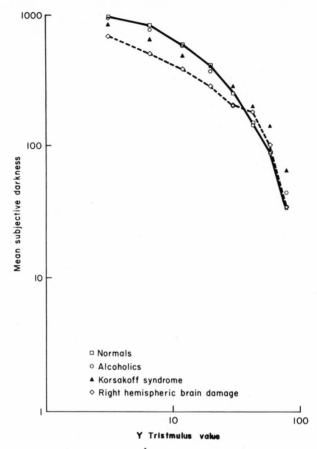

FIGURE 9.9 *The graph illustrates the group mean ratings of shades of gray, graphed on log–log coordinates.*

The results of the third study by Jones *et al.* (1978) replicated their previous reports concerning the scaling of butanol odor, loudness, and shades of gray by alcoholic Korsakoff patients. Although the alcoholic Korsakoff patients demonstrated normal intensity scaling of the shades of gray and the loudness of white noise, they were quite impaired in their olfactory scaling capacities and had elevated thresholds for the detection of butanol odor. Their correlation coefficients were lower than those of all other groups, indicating that their odor intensity ratings are less accurate than those of the other groups.

The most interesting new finding regarding the alcoholic Korsakoff group was the evidence of a deficit in the intensity scaling of salt solutions. Although alcoholic Korsakoff patients judged the two strongest salt solutions to be significantly weaker than did other subjects, they were not impaired in their overall ability to track the stimuli (i.e., their correlation coefficients were normal), and they had normal saline detection thresholds. However, their subnormal scaling of the strongest salt solutions confirmed the prediction of a gustatory deficit, made on the basis of damage to the VMN of the thalamus. It should be noted that because only 58% of patients with either or both components of the Wernicke-Korsakoff syndrome have lesions in the thalamic relay for the gustatory pathway, one would not expect their taste deficit to be as striking as their olfactory impairment.

The finding of a significant, although slight, abnormality in taste intensity scaling by alcoholic Korsakoff patients makes it appear even less likely that their olfactory deficits are due to olfactory bulb or olfactory nerve damage secondary to head trauma. Closed head injuries are very common in chronic alcoholics, and perhaps it could be argued that the alcoholic Korsakoff patients' olfactory problems are due to peripheral nerve damage, rather than to atrophy of diencephalic relay nuclei. Even if one were to accept such an explanation for their deficits in odor perception, head trauma could scarcely account for their abnormality in the scaling of taste intensities. Furthermore, the chronic long-term alcoholics in the Jones et al. studies were just as likely as the alcoholic Korsakoff patients to have sustained significant head trauma, yet, they were normal in their scaling of both olfactory and gustatory stimuli.

From the Jones et al. (1978) study, it is evident that brain-damaged (i.e., right-hemisphere) patients were impaired on all three visual tasks. Not only were these patients unable to scale the three types of visual material as accurately as other groups (as shown by their lower correlation coefficients), but they showed a reduced appreciation of stimuli at the upper end of each continuum. These findings suggest that the well known impairments of patients having right-hemispheric damage on higher-order visual and visuospatial tasks are mirrored on a more basic sensory level. It would seem that their visuoperceptual impairments are not limited to stimuli with a spatial or patterned component, but are apparent even on a task requiring brightness judgments.

In contrast to the prominent impairments of the brain-damaged patients on the three visual tasks, alcoholic Korsakoff patients evidenced only mild deficiencies on two of the visual measures. On the grid-complexity and circle-size scaling tasks, they had low correlations between stimulus intensity (i.e., size and complexity) and subjective ratings. Such results imply some deficit in the patients' accuracy of perception. The fact that the visual deficit was apparent only on the two tasks involving contour is consistent with our analyses of the alcoholic Korsakoff patients' visuoperceptual deficits. It will be remembered that these patients are often impaired on visuoperceptual tasks involving digit-symbol substitution and the identification of embedded figures (Glosser et al., 1977; Kapur & Butters, 1977; Talland, 1965), and that this impairment appears to be related to some deficiency in the patients' analyses of contours. Given such problems on complex perceptual tasks, perhaps it should not be surprising that these deficits are also seen, in an attenuated form, on relatively simple scaling tasks.

Finally, the Jones et al. (1978) findings provide no support for the contention that the impaired performance of alcoholic Korsakoff patients on olfactory (and gustatory) tasks is related to the complexity of these tasks and the general effects of brain damage. The demonstration that patients with right-hemispheric damage are severely impaired on the three visual-scaling tasks, but not on the olfactory or gustatory tasks, supports the conclusion of a special relationship between Korsakoff's syndrome and defects in the chemical senses. Given the neuropathology of Korsakoff's syndrome and the current knowledge of the neuroanatomical substrate of olfaction and gustation, it seems fair to conclude that diencephalic structures such as the MB, the VMN, and the MDN mediate some basic sensory functions, as well as the more advanced retentive and analytic capacities described in previous chapters of this book.

10

Memory and Cognitive Disorders
of Chronic Alcoholics

Korsakoff's syndrome has traditionally been considered an illness of acute onset (e.g., Victor, Adams, & Collins, 1971). The syndrome has been linked to a thiamine deficiency resulting from the alcoholics' poor dietary habits. As this thesis was discussed in Chapter 1, only a reminder that the etiology of this syndrome may be more complex than implied by the thiamine hypothesis is necessary here. The recent evidence suggesting that alcohol has a direct toxic effect on brain tissue (Freund, 1973; Riley & Walker, 1978) forces us to consider the possibility that Korsakoff's syndrome may be a chronic illness correlated with the degree and the length of alcohol abuse. Ryback (1971) has proposed such a continuity hypothesis and suggested that the alcoholic Korsakoff patient, the chronic alcoholic, and the heavy social drinker represent separate points along a single scale of cognitive impairment.

Continuities between alcoholic Korsakoff patients and long-term non-Korsakoff alcoholics have been demonstrated in numerous neuropsychological investigations. When contrasted with nonalcoholic control subjects, both chronic alcoholics and alcoholic Korsakoff patients perform poorly on visuoperceptual tasks requiring digit-symbol substitutions or the identification of embedded figures. On these tests, the scores of the chronic alcoholics fall midway between those of the alcoholic Korsakoff patients and the nonalcoholic control group (Glosser et al. 1977; Kapur & Butters, 1977). Similar continuities between alcoholic Korsakoff patients and chronic alcoholics have been demonstrated with complex visual problem-solving tasks. Oscar-Berman (1973) reported that alcoholic Korsakoff patients are more impaired than alcoholics on Levine's hypothesis-testing task. She found that the performance of both groups was inferior to that of neurologically intact control subjects and patients with Broca's aphasia. Also, alcoholics have been reported to be impaired on other visuoperceptual concept formation tasks, such as the Wisconsin Card Sorting Test (Tarter, 1973; Tarter & Parsons, 1971), the Halstead Category Test (Fitzhugh, Fitzhugh, & Reitan, 1965; Jones & Parsons, 1971), and the Advanced Form of Raven's Progressive Matrices (Jones, 1971). Kleinknecht and Goldstein (1972) and Goodwin and Hill (1975) have written extensive reviews documenting the chronic alcoholics' deficits on these various visuoperceptual and conceptual tasks.

Despite these demonstrations of a continuity between long-term alcoholics and alcoholic Korsakoff patients, the feature most characteristic of Korsakoff's syndrome is conspicuously absent from neuropsychological analyses of chronic non-Korsakoff alcoholics. Almost without exception, investigators have been unable to demonstrate the presence of a significant, relatively stable memory defect in *detoxified* alcoholics (for review, see Parsons & Prigatano, 1977). There are at least two plausible explanations for the failure to find verbal memory deficits in detoxified chronic alcoholics. One is that a permanent memory deficit only appears when alcoholism is combined with a chronic thiamine deficiency. Victor, Adams, and Collins (1971) have shown that atrophy of structures surrounding the third ventricle (i.e., the dorsomedial nucleus of the thalamus and/or the mammillary bodies) is the common denominator in Korsakoff's syndrome, and have postulated that thiamine deficiency is both necessary and sufficient to produce the syndrome. Because most chronic alcoholics may eat enough to maintain a sufficient level of thiamine, the short-term, verbal memory deficits associated with diencephalic–limbic damage may be apparent in only a small percentage of chronic alcoholics. A second possibility is that investigators have not utilized tests appropriate to gauging the alcoholics' verbal memory deficits. If the alcoholics' memory deficit is actually an attenuated form of the Korsakoff syndrome's retention disorder, then only specific tasks of sufficient complexity should differentiate long-term chronic alcoholics from short-term alcoholics and nonalcoholic control subjects. Determining whether this latter hypothesis is valid has not only theoretical significance but also practical value in the diagnosis and evaluation of alcoholics.

The results of three recent studies from our laboratory suggest that chronic alcoholics and alcoholic Korsakoff patients do share qualitatively similar anterograde memory problems. In the initial study,

When, after the first four trials, some of the control subjects were asked to describe the sorts of things they did to remember the words, they reported that they tried to form associations between the to-be-remembered words. For example, given the word pair *neck–salt,* a control subject volunteered, "I think of a neck, sweating, and the sweat is salty." Alcoholic subjects, on the other hand, were likely to say that they simply repeated the words to themselves, or that they did nothing special: "Neck–Salt . . . the words just don't go together." When other subjects were asked this same question after the second block of four trials, some alcoholics were able to describe relatively sophisticated associative mnemonics, which resulted in list mastery for a few of them.

The findings of this verbal, paired-associate learning study suggest that chronic alcoholics are processing information in a way that is different from that of nonalcoholics. Specifically, long-term alcoholics, like the alcoholic Korsakoff patients described in this book, seem less likely to spontaneously generate effective learning and remembering strategies.

Additional support for a learning deficit in chronic alcoholics was provided by the results of the symbol-digit, paired-associate learning test. This test (almost identical to the one used by Kapur and Butters, 1977) required the subject to associate seven single-digit numbers with seven unfamiliar geometric symbols, so that when each symbol was shown by itself the subject could provide the appropriate number. During the study phase, each symbol-digit pair was presented visually for 3 sec. After exposure to the entire seven-item list, the subject was presented with the symbol alone and asked to recall the number that had been associated with it. Each of the subject's responses was followed immediately by presentation of the correct symbol-digit pairing. Four test trials were administered, and the results can be seen in Figure 10.4. As anticipated, the performance of the alcoholic Korsakoff patients was severely impaired, with no indication of learning from trial to trial. The nonalcoholic control group, however, improved dramatically from the first to the fourth trial, and usually mastered the entire list. The long-term alcoholics also improved from trial to trial, but this improvement was slight. Although the alcoholics were impaired on the first test trial, the difference between the alcoholics and the normal controls increased with each test trial. Again, the alcoholics' learning scores were intermediate, falling between those of the alcoholic Korsakoff patients and the nonalcoholics.

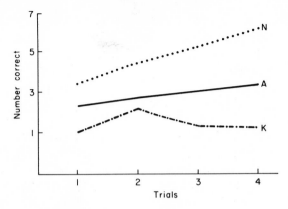

FIGURE 10.4 *The graphs illustrate the performance of normal controls (N), alco-holics (A), and alcoholic Korsakoff patients (K) on symbol-digit paired-associate learning task.*

The Peterson short-term memory test used by Ryan *et al.* (1980) increased the information-processing demands of this test by present-ing four, rather than three unrelated words on each trial, and by using retention intervals of 15 and 30 sec rather than the 3-, 9-, and 18-sec delays usually employed in our studies of alcoholic Korsakoff patients. On each trial four words (e.g., stain, lawn, cottage, angel) were read to the subject at the rate of one word per second. Following the presentation of the fourth word, the subject counted backward by threes from a given three-digit number. After 15 or 30 sec of counting, the examiner said "stop" and asked the subject to recall the four words previously presented. The performance of the three groups is shown in Figure 10.5. It is clear from this figure that as the retention interval was increased from 15 sec to 30 sec, the performance of each of these groups deteriorated. Of greater theoretical significance, however, are the differences between groups. The control group was superior to the long-term alcoholics and alcoholic Korsakoff patients, and the alcoholics were superior to the alcoholic Korsakoff patients. All three lines are parallel, a finding that would be predicted by Ryback's (1971) continuity hypothesis.

The Ryan *et al.* (1980) study suggests that long-term alcoholics with no clinically obvious cognitive impairments may have a subtle, but real, information-processing deficit that impairs their ability to learn and remember efficiently. This deficit was manifested on paired-associate learning and STM tasks. On both types of tests the alcoholic

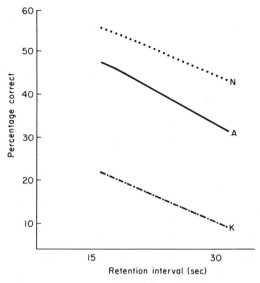

FIGURE 10.5 *The graphs illustrate the performance of nonalcoholic controls (N), alcoholics (A), and alcoholic Korsakoff patients (K) on verbal short-term memory task.*

Korsakoff patients evidenced the most severe impairments, but consistent with Ryback's (1971) continuum-of-impairment hypothesis, the chronic alcoholics obtained scores that fell between those of the alcoholic Korsakoff and the nonalcoholic control subjects. Informal assessments of the subjects' performance on paired-associate tasks also suggested that both chronic alcoholics and patients with Korsakoff's syndrome tended to employ developmentally primitive remembering (i.e., encoding) strategies.

If the continuity hypothesis is valid and the cognitive symptoms of Korsakoff's syndrome develop in a "chronic" rather than "acute" manner, one would expect to find a number of intermediate degrees of impairment. The test performance of a group of heavy social drinkers should be impaired relative to a group of occasional social drinkers, and the test performance of a group of alcoholics who complain of poor memory should be impaired relative to a group of alcoholics without memory complaints. Some empirical support has been provided for the first of these two predictions. In their study of upper-income social drinkers, Parker and Noble (1977) obtained significant negative correlations between performance on a variety of neuropsychological tests and the amount of alcohol consumed on each drinking occasion, and found this pattern more pronounced in heavy than in moderate drinkers.

In addition to supporting the idea that alcohol has a chronic neurotoxic effect upon the brain, the Ryan *et al.* findings also suggest that long-term alcohol abuse may induce a premature aging of the brain (Courville, 1966; Kleinknecht & Goldstein, 1972). As part of a cross-sectional investigation of the development of cognitive deficits, Ryan *et al.* tested a large number of 40- to 49-year-old alcoholics and 60- to 65-year-old nonalcoholics. Analyses of the resulting data indicated that the performance of the younger (40- to 49-year-old) alcoholics was identical to the performance of the older (50- to 59-year-old) nonalcoholics on all three of the described learning tasks. Similarly, the scores of the 50- to 59-year-old alcoholics was identical to the performance of the 60- to 65-year-old nonalcoholics. This is illustrated in Figure 10.6, which shows the performance of these groups on the first four trials of the verbal paired-associate learning test. Whether these sorts of parallels reflect the operation of identical underlying processes, or merely reflect the superficiality or grossness of the behavioral measures, is an intriguing but unresolved issue.

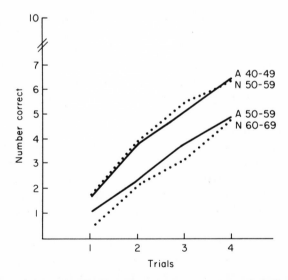

FIGURE 10.6 *The graphs illustrate the performance of nonalcoholic controls (N) between 50–59 and 60–65 years of age and of alcoholics (A) between 40–49 and 50–59 years of age on verbal paired-associate learning task.*

The demonstration that the anterograde amnesia of the alcoholic Korsakoff patient may develop slowly with sustained alcoholic abuse also raises some questions with regard to the course of these patients' retrograde amnesia. As noted several times in this text, alcoholic Korsakoff patients have difficulty recalling famous individuals and events from the remote past, and this memory deficit is characterized by a temporal gradient in which events and people from the earliest decades of the patients' lives are relatively preserved in comparison to events from recent decades. Although the empirical features of this retrograde amnesia are well established, little is known concerning the development of this symptom. One possibility, suggested by the Ryan et al. (1980) findings, is that the retrograde amnesia is an artifact related to a slowly progressing inability to learn new information. If the chronic alcoholic acquires less information each year due to an increasing deficit in information processing, then, at the time the patient is finally diagnosed as an "alcoholic Korsakoff," one would expect to find a retrograde amnesia with a temporal gradient. From this viewpoint, the alcoholic Korsakoff patient's retrograde amnesia may be considered secondary to a primary defect in establishing new memories (i.e., anterograde amnesia).

To assess this explanation of the retrograde problems of alcoholic Korsakoff patients, the retrograde amnesia battery developed by Albert et al. (1979a), and described in Chapter 1, was administered to a group of 15 long-term alcoholics (Albert, Butters, & Levin, 1980). Most of the alcoholics used in this study were the same individuals tested by Ryan et al. (1980) and therefore, had already demonstrated problems with learning new information.

Figure 10.7 shows the performance of the 15 chronic alcoholics, 17 nonalcoholic control subjects and 14 alcoholic Korsakoff patients on both the famous faces test and the recall questionnaire. The three groups were matched for age and educational background, and all of the chronic alcoholics had abused alcohol for more than 10 years, had been detoxified for a minimum of 30 days prior to testing, and met the general health standards described by Ryan et al. Statistical comparisons reflected what is evident from examination of the figure: There were no significant differences on these tests between the long-term alcoholics and the normal control subjects. The same result was also found on the multiple-choice questionnaire.

The results of this study have a number of implications for the relationship between alcohol abuse and remote memory. Deficits in

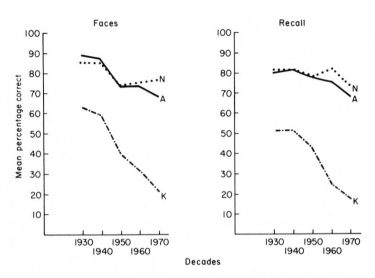

FIGURE 10.7 *The graphs illustrate the mean percentage correct on the Albert* et al. *Famous Faces Test and recall questionnaire (N = normal controls, A = alcoholics, K = alcoholic Korsakoff patients).*

remote memory (i.e., retrograde amnesia) do not appear to develop from a chronic inability to learn new materials, but seem to have an acute onset during the patient's Wernicke state. If the retrograde amnesia of the alcoholic Korsakoff patient is secondary to a chronic anterograde memory problem, some evidence of retrograde amnesia should have been noted in our group of long-term alcoholics. It appears then that although chronic alcoholics and alcoholic Korsakoff patients may share some of the same perceptual and short-term memory deficits, these continuities do not extend to difficulties in recalling remote events. Furthermore, based upon the previously noted comparisons of alcoholic Korsakoff and postencephalitic patients (Chapter 8), whatever neuroanatomical structures are acutely damaged in the alcoholic Korsakoff patient, they are likely to be different from those structures involved in the retrograde amnesia of postencephalitic patients.

The present findings also suggest that anterograde and retrograde amnesia involve different neural circuits and need not be associated with one another. Although alcoholic Korsakoffs clearly demonstrate both types of amnesia, non-Korsakoff alcoholics have some difficulty learning new information but are unimpaired in their recall of remote events and people. The fact that alcoholic Korsakoff and postencephalitic patients show a double dissociation on specific tests of new learning (Butters & Cermak, 1976) and remote memory lends further support to the separability of anterograde and retrograde memory problems. One should keep in mind, however, that the failure to demonstrate retrograde problems in chronic alcoholics may be a reflection of the level of complexity of the tests. A more difficult test of famous faces might have produced deficits consistent with the alcoholics' anterograde memory impairment.

Although it is not possible at this juncture to determine what neural circuits mediate anterograde and retrograde memory processes, a recent report based on stimulation studies with epileptic patients (Fedio & Van Buren, 1974) has produced evidence for such an anatomical separation. Two distinct areas concerned with memory were found within the left temporal lobe: Stimulation of the posterior region resulted in retrograde memory problems, whereas stimulation of the anterior region produced anterograde memory deficits. Because the amnesia of alcoholic Korsakoff patients is often attributed to atrophy of the dorsomedial nucleus of the thalamus (Victor *et al.,* 1971), a recent neuropathological report (Squire & Moore, 1979) concerning patient N.A. is of much interest. This patient, who is severely amnesic in his attempts to learn new verbal material but has only a mild retrograde deficit (Squire & Slater, 1978; Teuber, Milner, & Vaughn, 1968), appears to have unilateral destruction of the dorsomedial nucleus and no other visible damage. Therefore, one might speculate that the alcoholic Korsakoff patients' severe anterograde amnesia develops slowly due to the gradual atrophy of the dorsomedial nucleus, whereas their loss of remote memories appears suddenly with acute damage to other subcortical or cortical brain structures.

References

Aaronson, D. Temporal factors in perception and short-term memory. *Psychological Bulletin*, 1967, *67*, 130–144.

Adams, J. A. *Human memory*. New York: McGraw-Hill, 1967.

Adams, R. D., Collins, G. H., & Victor, M. Troubles de la mémoire et de l'apprentissage chez l'homme; leurs relations avec dés lesions des lobes temporaux et du diencéphale. In *Physiologie de l'Hippocampe*. Paris: Centre National de la Récherche Scientifique, 1962.

Albert, M. S., Butters, N., & Levin, J. Temporal gradients in the retrograde amnesia of patients with alcoholic Korsakoff's disease. *Archives of Neurology*, 1979, *36*, 211–216. (a)

Albert, M., Butters, N., & Levin, J. Memory for remote events in chronic alcoholics and alcoholic Korsakoff patients. In H. Begleiter & B. Kissin (Eds.), *Biological effects of alcohol*. New York: Plenum Press, 1980.

Atkinson, R. C., & Shiffrin, R. M. *Human Memory: A proposed system and its control processes* (Tech. Rep. 110). Stanford University, 1967.

Averbach, E., & Coriell, A. S. Short-term memory in vision. *Bell Systems Technical Journal*, 1961, *40*, 309–328.

Averbach, E., & Sperling, G. Short-term storage of information in vision. In C. Cherry (Ed.), *Information theory: Proceedings of the fourth London symposium*. London: Butterworth, 1961.

Baddeley, A. D. Short-term memory for word sequences as a function of acoustic, semantic and formal similarity. *Quarterly Journal of Experimental Psychology*, 1966, *18*, 362–365.

Baddeley, A. D. Estimating the short-term component in free recall. *British Journal of Psychology*, 1970, *61*, 13–15.

Baddeley, A. D. Theories of Amnesia. In A. Kennedy & A. Wilkes (Eds.), *Studies in long term memory*, New York: Wiley, 1975.

Baddeley, A. D., & Dale, H. C. A. The effect of semantic similarity on retroactive interference in long- and short-term memory. *Journal of Verbal Learning and Verbal Behavior*, 1966, *5*, 417–420.

Baddeley, A. D., & Warrington, E. K. Amnesia and the distinction between long- and short-term memory. *Journal of Verbal Learning and Verbal Behavior*, 1970, *9*, 176–189.

Baddeley, A. D., & Warrington, E. K. Memory coding and amnesia. *Neuropsychologia*, 1973, *11*, 159–165.

Bahrick, H. P. Measurement of memory by prompted recall. *Journal of Experimental Psychology*, 1969, *79*, 213–219.

Barnes, J. B., & Underwood, B. J. "Fate" of first-list associations in transfer theory. *Journal of Experimental Psychology*, 1959, *58*, 97–105.

Benson, D. F., & Geschwind, N. Shrinking retrograde amnesia. *Journal of Neurology, Neurosurgery, and Psychiatry*, 1967, *30*, 539–544.

Benton, A. L., & Van Allen, N. W. Impairment in facial recognition in patients with cerebral disease. *Cortex*, 1968, *4*, 344–358.

Bransford, J. D., McCarrell, N. S., Franks, J. J., & Nitsch, K. E. Toward unexplaining memory. In R. E. Shaw & J. D. Bransford (Eds.), *Perceiving, acting, and knowing: Toward an ecological psychology*. Hillsdale, New Jersey: Lawrence Erlbaum, 1977.

Bransford, J. D., Franks, J. J., Morris, C. D., & Stein, B. S. Some general constraints on learning and memory research. In L. S. Cermak & F. I. M. Craik (Eds.), *Levels of processing in human memory*. Hillsdale, New Jersey: Lawrence Erlbaum, 1979.

Bregman, A. S. Forgetting curves with semantic, phonetic, graphic, and contiguity cues. *Journal of Experimental Psychology*, 1968, *78*, 539–546.

Brewer, C., & Perrett, L. Brain damage due to alcohol consumption: An airencephalographic, psychometric, and electroencephalographic study. *British Journal of Addiction*, 1971, *60*, 170–182.

Brierly, J. B. Neuropathology of amnesic states. In C. W. M. Whitty & O. L. Zangwill (Eds.), *Amnesia* (2nd ed.). Boston: Butterworths, 1977.

Briggs, B. E. Acquisition, extinction, and recovery functions in retroactive inhibition. *Journal of Experimental Psychology*, 1954, *47*, 285–293.

Broadbent, D. E. *Perception and communication*. London: Pergamon, 1958.

Burton, H., & Benjamin, R. M. Central projections of the gustatory system. In L. M. Beidler (Ed.), *Handbook of sensory physiology* (Vol. 4). New York: Springer-Verlag, 1971.

Butters, N., Albert, M. S., & Sax, D. Investigations of the memory disorders of patients with Huntington's Disease. In T. Chase, N. Wexler, & A. Barbeau (Eds.), *Advances in neurology, Volume 23, Huntington's Disease.* New York: Raven, 1979.

Butters, N., & Cermak, L. S. Neuropsychological studies of alcoholic Korsakoff patients. In G. Goldstein & C. Neuringer (Eds.), *Empirical studies of alcoholism*. Cambridge, Massachusetts: Ballinger, 1976.

Butters, N., Cermak, L. S., Montgomery, K., & Adinolfi, A. Some comparisons of the memory and visuoperceptive deficits of chronic alcoholics and patients with Korsakoff's disease. *Alcoholism: Clinical and Experimental Research*, 1977, *1*, 73–80.

Butters, N., & Grady, M. Effect of predistractor delays on the short-term memory performance of patients with Korsakoff's and Huntington's disease. *Neuropsychologia*, 1977, *15*, 701–706.

Butters, N., Tarlow, S., Cermak, L. S., & Sax, D. A comparison of the information processing deficits of patients with Huntington's Chorea and Korsakoff's syndrome. *Cortex*, 1976, *12*, 134–144.

Caine, E. D., Ebert, M. H., & Weingartner, H. An outline for the analysis of dementia: The memory disorder of Huntington's disease. *Neurology*, 1977, *27*, 1087–1092.

Carey, S., & Diamond, R. From piecemeal to configurational representation of faces. *Science*, 1977, *195*, 312–314.

Cermak, L. S. *Human memory: Research and theory*. New York: Ronald Press, 1972.

Cermak, L. S. Imagery as an aid to retrieval for Korsakoff patients. *Cortex*, 1975, *11*, 163–169.

Cermak, L. S. The encoding capacity of a patient with amnesia due to encephalitis. *Neuropsychologia*, 1976, *14*, 311–326.

Cermak, L. S. The contribution of a "processing" deficit to alcoholic Korsakoff patients' memory disorder. In I. M. Birnbaum & E. S. Parker (Eds.), *Alcohol and human memory*. Hillsdale, New Jersey: Lawrence Erlbaum, 1977.

Cermak, L. S., & Butters, N. The role of interference and encoding in the short-term memory deficits of Korsakoff patients. *Neuropsychologia*, 1972, *10*, 89–96.

Cermak, L. S., & Butters, N. The role of language in the memory disorders of brain damaged patients. *Annals of the New York Academy of Science*, 1976, *280*, 857–867.

Cermak, L. S., Butters, N., & Gerrein, J. The extent of the verbal encoding ability of Korsakoff patients. *Neuropsychologia*, 1973, *11*, 85–94.

Cermak, L. S., Butters, N., & Goodglass, H. The extent of memory loss in Korsakoff patients. *Neuropsychologia*, 1971, *9*, 307–315.

Cermak, L. S., Butters, N., & Moreines, J. Some analyses of the verbal encoding deficit of alcoholic Korsakoff patients. *Brain and Language*, 1974, *1*, 141–150.

Cermak, L. S., Lewis, R., Butters, N., & Goodglass, H. Role of verbal mediation in performance of motor tasks by Korsakoff patients. *Perceptual and Motor Skills*, 1973, *37*, 259–262.

Cermak, L. S., & Moreines, J. Verbal retention deficits in aphasic and amnesic patients. *Brain and Language*, 1976, *3*, 16–27.

Cermak, L. S., Naus, M. J., & Reale, L. Rehearsal and organizational strategies of alcoholic Korsakoff patients. *Brain and Language*, 1976, *3*, 375–385.

Cermak, L. S., & Reale, L. Depth of processing and retention of words by alcoholic Korsakoff patients. *Journal of Experimental Psychology: Human Learning and Memory*, 1978, *4*, 165–174.

Cermak, L. S., Reale, L., & Baker, E. Alcoholic Korsakoff patients' retrieval from semantic memory. *Brain and Language*, 1978, *5*, 215–226.

Cermak, L. S., Reale, L., & DeLuca, D. Korsakoff patients' nonverbal versus verbal memory: Effects of interference and mediation on rate of information loss. *Neuropsychologia*, 1977, *15*, 303–310.

Cermak, L. S., & Tarlow, S. Aphasic and amnesic patients' verbal versus nonverbal retentive abilities. *Cortex*, 1978, *14*, 32–40.

Cermak, L. S., & Uhly, B. Short-term motor memory in Korsakoff patients. *Perceptual and Motor Skills*, 1975, *40*, 275–281.

Cermak, L. S., & Youtz, C. *Differential resistance to interference of acoustic and semantic encoding*. Paper presented at the Psychonomic Society Convention, Boston, November 1974.

Chorover, S. L., & Schiller, P. H. Short-term retrograde amnesia in rats. *Journal of Comparative and Physiological Psychology*, 1965, *59*, 73–78.

Clark, S. E. Retrieval of color information from preperceptual memory. *Journal of Experimental Psychology*, 1969, *82*, 263–266.

Collins, A. M., & Loftus, E. F. A spreading-activation theory of semantic processing. *Psychological Review*, 1975, *82*, 407–428.

Conrad, R. An association between memory errors and errors due to acoustic masking of speech. *Nature*, 1962, *196*, 1314–1315.

Conrad, R. Acoustic confusions in immediate memory. *British Journal of Psychology*, 1964, *55*, 75–84.

Cooper, E. H., & Pantle, A. J. The total-time hypothesis in verbal learning. *Psychological Bulletin*, 1967, *68*, 221–234.

Corkin, S. Acquisition of motor skill after bilateral medial temporal-lobe excision. *Neuropsychologia*, 1968, *6*, 255–265.

Courville, C. B. *Effects of alcohol on the nervous system of man.* Los Angeles: San Lucas Press, 1966.

Craik, F. I. M. Conclusions and comments. In L. S. Cermak & F .I. M. Craik (Eds.), *Levels of processing in human memory.* Hillsdale, New Jersey: Lawrence Erlbaum, 1979.

Craik, F. I. M., & Lockhart, R. S. Levels of processing: A framework for memory research. *Journal of Verbal Learning and Verbal Behavior*, 1972, *11*, 671–684.

Craik, F. I. M., & Masani, P. A. Age and intelligence differences in coding and retrieval of word lists. *British Journal of Psychology*, 1969, *60*, 315–319.

Craik, F. I. M., & Tulving, E. Depth of processing and retention of words in episodic memory. *Journal of Experimental Psychology, General*, 1975, *104*, 268–294.

Crowder, R. G., & Morton, J. Precategorical acoustic storage. *Perception and Psychophysics*, 1969, *5*, 365–373.

Delay, J., Brion, S., & Elissalde, B. Corps mamillaires et syndrome Korsakoff. Etude anatomique de huit cas de syndrome de Korsakoff d'origine alcoolique sans alterations significative du cortex cerebral. I. Etude anatomo-clinique. *L'Presse Medicale*, 1958, *66*, 1849–1852. (a)

Delay, J., Brion, S., & Elissalde, B. Corps mamillaires et syndrome Korsakoff. Etude anatomique de huit cas de syndrome de Korsakoff d'origine alcoolique sans alterations significative due cortex cerebral. II. Tubercules mamillaires et mecanisme de la memoire. *L'Presse Medicale*, 1958, *66*, 1965–1968. (b)

DeLuca, D., Cermak, L. S., & Butters, N. The differential effects of semantic, acoustic, and nonverbal distraction on Korsakoff patients' verbal retention performance. *International Journal of Neuroscience*, 1976, *6*, 279–284.

DeRenzi, G., & Spinnler, H. Facial recognition in brain-damaged patients. *Neurology*, 1966, *16*, 145–152.

Dick, A. O. Relations between the sensory register and short-term storage in tachistoscopic recognition. *Journal of Experimental Psychology*, 1969, *82*, 279–284.

Drachman, D. A., & Adams, R. D. Herpes Simplex and acute inclusion body encephalitis. *Archives of Neurology*, 1962, *7*, 45–63.

Drachman, D. A., & Arbit, J. Memory and the hippocampal complex. *Archives of Neurology*, 1966, *15*, 52–61.

Dreyfus, P. M. Diseases of the nervous system in chronic alcoholics. In B. Kissin & H. Begleiter (Eds.), *The biology of alcoholism: Clinical pathology* (Vol. 3). New York: Plenum, 1974.

Dricker, J., Butters, N., Berman, G., Samuels, I., & Carey, S. Recognition and encoding of faces by alcoholic Korsakoff and right hemisphere patients. *Neuropsychologia*, 1978, *16*, 683–695.

Epstein, P. S., Pisani, D., & Fawcett, J. A. Alcoholism and cerebral atrophy. *Alcoholism: Clinical and Experimental Research*, 1977, *1*, 61–65.

Fedio, P., & Van Buren, J. M. Memory deficits during electrical stimulation in the speech cortex of conscious man. *Brain and Language*, 1974, *1*, 29–42.

Fisher, R. P., & Craik, F. I. M. The interaction between encoding and retrieval operations in cued recall. *Journal of Experimental Psychology: Human Learning and Memory*, 1977, *3*, 701–711.

Fitzhugh, L. C., Fitzhugh, K. B., & Reitan, R. M. Adaptive abilities and intellectual functioning of hospitalized alcoholics: Further considerations. *Quarterly Journal of Studies on Alcohol*, 1965, *26*, 402–411.

Flexner, J. B., Flexner, L. B., & Stellar, E. Memory in mice as affected by intracerebral puromycin. *Science*, 1963, *141*, 57–59.

Fox, J. H., Ramsey, R. G., Huckman, M. S., & Proske, A. E. Cerebral ventricular enlargement. Chronic alcoholics examined by computerized tomography. *Journal of the American Medical Association*, 1976, *256*, 365–368.

Freedman, J. L., & Loftus, E. F. Retrieval of words from long-term memory. *Journal of Verbal Learning and Verbal Behavior*, 1971, *10*, 107–115.

Freund, G. Impairment of shock avoidance learning after long-term alcohol ingestion in mice. *Science*, 1970, *168*, 1599–1601.

Freund, G. Chronic central nervous system toxicity of alcohol. *Annual Review of Pharmacology*, 1973, *13*, 217–227.

Freund, G., & Walker, D. W. Impairment of avoidance learning by prolonged ethanol consumption in mice. *Journal of Pharmacology and Experimental Therapeutics*, 1971, *179*, 284–292.

Gamper, E. Zur frage der Polioencephalitis haemorrhagic der chronischen Alkoholiker. Anatomische Befunde beim alkoholischen Korsakov und ihre Beziehungen zum klinischen Bild. *Deutsche Zeitschrift Fuer Nervenheilkunde*, 1928, *102*, 122–129.

Glanzer, M., & Cunitz, A. R. Two storage mechanisms in free recall. *Journal of Verbal Learning and Verbal Behavior*, 1966, *5*, 351–360.

Glosser, G., Butters, N., & Kaplan, E. Visuoperceptual processes in brain-damaged patients on the digit symbol substitution tests. *International Journal of Neuroscience*, 1977, *7*, 59–66.

Glosser, G., Butters, N., & Samuels, I. Failures in information processing in patients with Korsakoff's syndrome. *Neuropsychologia*, 1976, *14*, 327–334.

Goldman, P. S. Role of experience in recovery of function following orbital prefrontal lesions in infant monkeys. *Neuropsychologia*, 1976, *14*, 401–442.

Goldstein, G. Perceptual and cognitive deficits in alcoholics. In G. Goldstein & C. Neuringer (Eds.), *Empirical studies of alcoholism*. Cambridge: Ballinger, 1976.

Goldstein, G., & Shelly, C. H. Field dependence and cognitive, perceptual and motor skills in alcoholics. *Quarterly Journal of Studies on Alcohol*, 1971, *32*, 29–40.

Goodwin, D. W., & Hill, S. Y. Chronic effects of alcohol and other psychoactive drugs on intellect, learning, and memory. In J. Rankin (Ed.), *Alcohol, drugs, and brain damage*. Ontario: Addiction Research Foundation, 1975.

Haber, R. N. How we remember what we see. *Scientific American*, 1970, *1*, 149–156.

Hebb, D. O. *The organization of behavior*. New York: Wiley, 1949.

Huppert, F. A., & Piercy, M. Recognition memory in amnesic patients: Effects of temporal context and familiarity of material. *Cortex*, 1976, *12*, 3–20.

Huppert, F. A., & Piercy, M. Recognition memory in amnesic patients: A defect of acquisition? *Neuropsychologia*, 1977, *15*, 643–652.

Huppert, F. A., & Piercy, M. Dissociation between learning and remembering in organic amnesia. *Nature*, 1978, *275*, 317–318.

Hyde, T. S., & Jenkins, J. J. Recall for words as a function of semantic, graphic, and syntactic orienting tasks. *Journal of Verbal Learning and Verbal Behavior*, 1973, *12*, 471–480.

Jarho, L. *Korsakoff-like amnesic syndrome in penetrating brain injury*. Helsinki: Rehabilitation Institute for Brain Injured Veterans in Finland, 1973.

Jenkins, J. J. Four points to remember: A tetrahedral model of memory experiments. In L. S. Cermak & F. I. M. Craik (Eds.), *Levels of processing in human memory*. Hillsdale, New Jersey: Lawrence Erlbaum, 1979.

Jones, B. P., Butters, N., Moskowitz, H. R., & Montgomery, K. Olfactory and gustatory capacities of alcoholic Korsakoff patients. *Neuropsychologia*, 1978, *16*, 323–337.

Jones, B. P., Moskowitz, H. R., & Butters, N. Olfactory discrimination in alcoholic Korsakoff patients. *Neuropsychologia*, 1975, *13*, 173–179. (a)

Jones, B. P., Moskowitz, H. R., Butters, N., & Glosser, G. Psychophysical scaling of olfactory, visual, and auditory stimuli by alcoholic Korsakoff patients. *Neuropsychologia*, 1975, *13*, 387–393. (b)

Jones, B. Verbal and spatial intelligence in short- and long-term alcoholics. *Journal of Nervous and Mental Disease*, 1971, *153*, 292–297.

Jones, B., & Parsons, O. A. Impaired abstracting ability in chronic alcoholics. *Archives of General Psychiatry*, 1971, *24*, 71–75.

Kapur, N., & Butters, N. An analysis of the visuoperceptual deficits in alcoholic Korsakoffs and long-term alcoholics. *Journal of Studies on Alcohol*, 1977, *38*, 2025–2035.

Keppel, G., & Underwood, B. J. Proactive inhibition in short-term retention of single items. *Journal of Verbal Learning and Verbal Behavior*, 1962, *1*, 153–161.

Kinsbourne, M., & Wood, F. Short-term memory processes and the amnesic syndrome. In D. Deutsch & J. A. Deutsch (Eds.), *Short-term memory*. New York: Academic Press, 1975.

Kintsch, W. *Learning, memory, and conceptual processes*. New York: Wiley, 1970.

Kleinknecht, R. A., & Goldstein, S. G. Neuropsychological deficits associated with alcoholism. *Quarterly Journal of Studies on Alcohol*, 1972, *33*, 999–1019.

Kolers, P. A. Specificity of operations in sentence recognition. *Cognitive Psychology*, 1975, *7*, 289–306.

Kolers, P. A. A pattern analyzing basis of recognition. In L. S. Cermak & F. I. M. Craik (Eds.), *Levels of processing in human memory*. Hillsdale, New Jersey: Lawrence Erlbaum, 1979.

Kroll, N. E. A., Parks, T., Parkinson, S. R., Bieber, S. L., & Johnson, A. L. Short-term memory while shadowing. Recall of visually and aurally presented letters. *Journal of Experimental Psychology*, 1970, *85*, 220–224.

Lachman, J. L., & Lachman, R. Comprehension and cognition: A state of the art inquiry. In L. S. Cermak & F. I. M. Craik (Eds.), *Levels of processing in human memory*. Hillsdale, New Jersey: Lawrence Erlbaum, 1979.

Levy, B. A. Role of articulation in auditory and visual short-term memory. *Journal of Verbal Learning and Verbal Behavior,* 1971, *10,* 123–132.

Lhermitte, F., & Signoret, J. L. Neurological analysis and differentiation of amnesic syndromes. *Revue Neurologique,* 1972, *126,* 161–178.

Loftus, E. F. *How to catch a zebra in semantic memory.* Paper presented at the Minnesota Conference on Cognition, Knowledge, and Adaptation, Minneapolis, 1973. (a)

Loftus, E. F. Activation of semantic memory. *American Journal of Psychology,* 1973, *86,* 331–337. (b)

MacLeod, P. Structure and function of higher olfactory centers. In L. M. Beidler (Ed.), *Handbook of sensory physiology* (Vol. 4). New York: Springer-Verlag. 1971.

Marslen-Wilson, W. D., & Teuber, H. L. Memory for remote events in anterograde amnesia: Recognition of public figures from news photographs. *Neuropsychologia,* 1975, *13,* 347–352.

McGeoch, J. A. Forgetting and the law of disuse. *Psychological Review,* 1932, *39,* 352–370.

Melton, A. W. Implications of short-term memory for a general theory of memory. *Journal of Verbal Learning and Verbal Behavior,* 1963, *2,* 1–21.

Melton, A. W., & Irwin, J. The influence of degree of interpolated learning on retroactive inhibition and the overt transfer of specific responses. *American Journal of Psychology,* 1940, *53,* 173–203.

Mesulam, M., Van Hoesen, G., & Butters, N. Clinical manifestations of chronic thiamine deficiency in the rhesus monkey. *Neurology,* 1977, *27,* 239–245.

Miller, E. *Abnormal aging: The psychology of senile and presenile dementia.* London: Wiley, 1977.

Miller, G. A. The magical number seven, plus or minus two: Some limits on our capacity for processing information. *Psychological Review,* 1956, *63,* 81–97.

Milner, B. The memory defect in bilateral hippocampal lesions. *Psychiatric Research Reports,* 1959, *11,* 43–52.

Milner, B. Amnesia following operation on the temporal lobes. In C. W. M. Whitty & O. L. Zangwill (Eds.), *Amnesia.* London: Butterworths, 1966.

Milner, B. Brain mechanisms suggested by studies of temporal lobes. In F. L. Darley (Ed.), *Brain mechanisms underlying speech and language.* New York: Grune & Stratton, 1967.

Milner, B., Visual recognition and recall after right temporal-lobe excision in man. *Neuropsychologia,* 1968, *6,* 191–209.

Milner, B. Memory and the medial temporal regions of the brain. In K. H. Pribram & D. E. Broadbent (Eds.), *Biology of memory.* New York: Academic Press, 1970.

Milner, B., Corkin, S., & Teuber, H. L. Further analysis of the hippocampal amnesic syndrome: 14-year follow-up study of H. M. *Neuropsychologia,* 1968, *6,* 215–234.

Moray, N. Attention in dichotic listening: Affective cues and the influence of instructions. *Quarterly Journal of Experimental Psychology,* 1959, *11,* 56–60.

Muedell, P., Butters, N., & Montgomery, K. Role of rehearsal in the short-term memory performance of patients with Korsakoff's and Huntington's Disease. *Neuropsychologia,* 1978, *16,* 507–510.

Murdock, B. B., Jr. The retention of individual items. *Journal of Experimental Psychology,* 1961, *62,* 525–632.

Murdock, B. B., Jr. The serial position effect in free recall. *Journal of Experimental Psychology*, 1962, *64*, 482–488.

Murdock, B. B., Jr. Recent developments in short-term memory. *British Journal of Psychology*, 1967, *58*, 421–433.

Murdock, B. B., Jr. Four channel effects in short-term memory. *Psychonomic Science*, 1971, *24*, 197–198.

Murdock, B. B., Jr. Short-term memory. In G. H. Bower (Ed.), *Psychology of learning and motivation* (Vol. 5). New York: Academic Press, 1972.

Naus, M. J., Cermak, L. S., & DeLuca, D. Retrieval processes in alcoholic Korsakoff patients. *Neuropsychologia*, 1977, *15*, 737–742.

Neisser, U. *Cognitive Psychology*. New York: Appleton-Century-Crofts, 1967.

Nelson, D. L. Remembering pictures and words: Appearance, significance, and name. In L. S. Cermak & F. I. M. Craik (Eds.), *Levels of processing in human memory*. Hillsdale, New Jersey: Lawrence Erlbaum, 1979.

O'Keefe, J., & Nadel, L. *The Hippocampus as a cognitive map*. London: Oxford Univ. Press, 1978.

Oscar-Berman, M. Hypothesis testing and focusing behavior during concept formation by amnesic Korsakoff patients. *Neuropsychologia*, 1973, *11*, 191–198.

Oscar-Berman, M., Goodglass, H., & Cherlow, D. G. Perceptual laterality and iconic recognition of visual materials by Korsakoff patients and normal adults. *Journal of Comparative and Physiological Psychology*, 1973, *82*, 316–321.

Oscar-Berman, M., & Samuels, I. Stimulus preference and memory factors in Korsakoff's syndrome. *Neuropsychologia*, 1977, *15*, 99–106.

Paivio, A. *Imagery and verbal processes*. New York: Holt, Rinehart and Winston, 1971.

Paivio, A. Imagery and Language. In S. J. Segal (Ed.), *Imagery: Current cognitive approaches*. New York: Academic Press, 1971.

Parker, E. S., & Noble, E. Alcohol consumption and cognitive functioning in social drinkers. *Journal of Studies on Alcohol*, 1977, *38*, 1224–1232.

Parsons, O. A. Brain damage in alcoholics: altered states of unconsciousness. In M. Gross (Ed.), *Alcohol intoxication and withdrawal II*. New York: Plenum Press, 1975.

Parsons, O. A., & Prigatano, G. P. Memory functioning in alcoholics. In I. M. Birnbaum & E. S. Parker (Eds.), *Alcohol and human memory*. Hillsdale, New Jersey: Lawrence Erlbaum, 1977.

Parsons, O. A., Tarter, R. E., & Jones, B. Cognitive deficits in chronic alcoholics. *Il Lavoro Neuro Psichiatrico*, 1971, *49*, 5–14.

Pearlman, C. A., Sharpless, S. K., & Jarvick, M. I. Retrograde amnesia produced by anesthetic and convulsant agents. *Journal of Comparative and Physiological Psychology*, 1961, *54*, 109.

Peterson, L. R., & Johnson, S. T. Some effects of minimizing articulation on short-term retention. *Journal of Verbal Learning and Verbal Behavior*, 1971, *10*, 346–354.

Peterson, L. R., & Peterson, M. J. Short-term retention of individual verbal items. *Journal of Experimental Psychology*, 1959, *58*, 193–198.

Phillips, W. A., & Baddeley, A. D. Reaction time and short-term visual memory. *Psychonomic Science*, 1971, *22*, 73–74.

Piercy, M. F. Experimental studies of the organic amnesic syndrome. In C. W. M. Whitty & O. L. Zangwill (Eds.), *Amnesia* (2nd ed). London: Butterworths, 1977.

Posner, M. I. Short-term memory systems in human information processing. *Acta Psychologia*, 1967, *27*, 267–284.

Posner, M. I. Abstraction and the powers of recognition. In G. H. Bower & J. T. Spence (Eds.), *The psychology of learning and motivation: Advances in research and theory* (Vol. 3). New York: McGraw-Hill, 1969.

Prisko, L. Short-term memory in focal cerebral damage. Unpublished doctoral dissertation, McGill University, 1963.

Riggs, H. E., & Boles, H. S. Wernicke's disease: A clinical and pathological study of 42 cases. *Quarterly Journal of Studies on Alcohol*, 1944, *5*, 361–370.

Riley, J. N., & Walker, D. W. Morphological alterations in hippocampus after long-term alcohol consumption in mice. *Science*, 1978, *201*, 646–648.

Rundus, D., & Atkinson, R. C. Rehearsal processes in free recall: A procedure for direct observation. *Journal of Verbal Learning and Verbal Behavior*, 1970, *9*, 99–105.

Runquist, W. N., Verbal behavior. In J. B. Sidowski (Ed.), *Experimental methods and instrumentation in psychology*. New York: McGraw-Hill, 1966.

Ryan, C., Butters, N., Montgomery, K., Adinolfi, A., & Didario, B. Memory deficits in chronic alcoholics: Continuities between the "intact" alcoholic and the alcoholic Korsakoff patient. In H. Begleiter & B. Kissin (Eds.), *Biological effects of alcohol*. New York: Plenum, 1980.

Ryback, R. The continuum and specificity of the effects of alcohol on memory. *Quarterly Journal of Studies on Alcohol*, 1971, *32*, 995–1016.

Samuels, I., Butters, N., & Goodglass, H. Visual memory deficits following cortical and limbic lesions: Effect of field of presentation. *Physiology and Behavior*, 1971, *6*, 447–452.

Samuels, I., Butters, N., Goodglass, H., & Brody, B. A comparison of subcortical and cortical damage on short-term visual and auditory memory. *Neuropsychologia*, 1971, *9*, 293–306.

Sanders, H. I., & Warrington, E. K. Memory for remote events in amnesic patients. *Brain*, 1971, *94*, 661–668.

Scoville, W. B., & Milner, B. Loss of recent memory after bilateral hippocampal lesions. *Neuropsychologia*, 1957, *20*, 11–21.

Seltzer, B., & Benson, D. F. The temporal pattern of retrograde amnesia in Korsakoff's disease. *Neurology*, 1974, *24*, 527–530.

Shepard, R. N. Recognition memory for words, sentences, and pictures. *Journal of Verbal Learning and Verbal Behavior*, 1967, *6*, 156–163.

Shulman, H. G. Encoding and retention of semantic and phonemic information in short-term memory. *Journal of Verbal Learning and Verbal Behavior*, 1970, *9*, 499–508.

Sidman, M., Stoddard, L. T., & Mohr, J. P. Some additional quantitative observations of immediate memory in a patient with bilateral hippocampal lesions. *Neuropsychologia*, 1968, *6*, 245–254.

Sperling, G. The information available in brief visual presentations. *Psychological Monographs*, 1960, *74* (Whole No. 498).

Squire, L. R. A stable impairment in remote memory following electro-convulsive therapy. *Neuropsychologia*, 1975, *13*, 51–58.

Squire, L. R., & Moore, R. Y. Dorsal thalamic lesions in a noted case of chronic memory dysfunction. *Annals of Neurology*, 1979, *6*, 503–506.

Squire, L. R., Slater, P. C., & Chace, P. M. Retrograde amnesia: Temporal gradient in very long term memory following electro-convulsive therapy. *Science*, 1975, *187*, 77–79.

Squire, L. R., & Slater, P. C. Anterograde and retrograde memory impairment in chronic amnesia. *Neuropsychologia*, 1978, *16*, 313–322.

Sternberg, S. High speed scanning in human memory. *Science*, 1966, *153*, 652–654.

Stoff, M., & Eagle, M. N. The relationship among reported strategies, presentation rate, and verbal ability and their effects on free recall learning. *Journal of Experimental Psychology*, 1971, *87*, 423–428.

Talland, G. *Deranged memory*. New York: Academic Press, 1965.

Tarter, R. E. An analysis of cognitive deficits in chronic alcoholics. *Journal of Nervous and Mental Disease*, 1973, *157*, 138–147.

Tarter, R. E., & Parsons, O. A. Conceptual shifting in chronic alcoholics. *Journal of Abnormal Psychology*, 1971, *77*, 71–75.

Taylor, R. L. Comparison of short-term memory and visual sensory analysis as sources of information. *Journal of Experimental Psychology*, 1969, *81*, 515–522.

Teuber, H. L., Milner, B., & Vaughan, H. G., Jr. Persistent anterograde amnesia after stab wound of the basal brain. *Neuropsychologia*, 1968, *6*, 267–282.

Thomson, D. M., & Tulving, E. Associative encoding and retrieval: Weak and strong cues. *Journal of Experimental Psychology*, 1970, *86*, 255–262.

Thorndike, E. L. *Educational psychology*. New York: Teachers College Press, Columbia Univ., 1913.

Till, R. E., & Jenkins, J. J. The effects of cued orienting tasks on the free recall of words. *Journal of Verbal Learning and Verbal Behavior*, 1973, *12*, 489–498.

Treisman, A. Monitoring and storage of irrelevant messages in selective attention. *Journal of Verbal Learning and Verbal Behavior*, 1964, *3*, 449–459.

Tulving, E. The effect of alphabetical subjective organization on memorizing unrelated words. *Canadian Journal of Psychology*, 1962, *16*, 185–191.

Tulving, E. Short- and long-term memory: Different retrieval mechanisms. In K. H. Pribram & D. Broadbent (Eds.), *Biology of memory*. New York: Academic Press, 1970.

Tulving, E. Episodic and semantic memory. In E. Tulving & W. Donaldson (Eds.), *Organization of memory*. New York: Academic Press, 1972.

Tulving, E. Relations between encoding and levels of processing. In L. S. Cermak & F. I. M. Craik (Eds.), *Levels of processing in human memory*. Hillsdale, New Jersey: Lawrence Erlbaum, 1979.

Underwood, B. J. False recognition by implicit verbal response. *Journal of Experimental Psychology*, 1965, *70*, 122–129.

Victor, M., Adams, R. D., & Collins, G. H. *The Wernicke-Korsakoff syndrome*. Philadelphia: F. A. Davis, 1971.

Walker, D. W., & Freund, G. Impairment of shuttle box avoidance learning following prolonged alcohol consumption in rats. *Physiology and Behavior*, 1971, *7*, 773–778.

Walsh, D. A., & Jenkins, J. J. Effects of orienting tasks on free recall in incidental learning: "Difficulty," "effort," and "process" explanations. *Journal of Verbal Learning and Verbal Behavior*, 1973, *12*, 481–488.

179

Warrington, E. K. Constructional apraxia. In P. J. Vinken & G. W. Bruyn (Eds.), *Handbook of clinical neurology* (Vol. 4). Amsterdam: North Holland, 1969.

Warrington, E. K., & James, M. An experimental investigation of facial recognition in patients with unilateral cerebral lesions. *Cortex*, 1967, *3*, 317–326.

Warrington, E. K., & Shallice, T. The selective impairment of auditory verbal short-term memory. *Brain*, 1969, *92*, 885–896.

Warrington, E. K., & Weiskrantz, L. A study of learning and retention in amnesic patients. *Neuropsychologia*, 1968, *228*, 628–630. (a)

Warrington, E. K., & Weiskrantz, L. New method of testing long-term retention with special reference to amnesic patients. *Nature*, 1968, *217*, 972–974. (b)

Warrington, E. K., & Weiskrantz, L. Amnesic syndrome: Consolidation or retrieval? *Nature*, 1970, *228*, 628–630.

Warrington, E. K., & Weiskrantz, L. Organizational aspects of memory in amnesic patients. *Neuropsychologia*, 1971, *9*, 67–73.

Warrington, E. K., & Weiskrantz, L. An analysis of short-term and long-term memory defects in man. In J. A. Deutsch (Ed.), *The physiological basis of memory*. New York: Academic Press, 1973.

Warrington, E. K., & Weiskrantz, L. Further analysis of the prior learning effect in amnesic patients. *Neuropsychologia*, 1978, *16*, 169–177.

Waugh, N. C., & Barr, R. *Memory and mental tempo*. Paper presented at the George Talland Memorial Conference on Aging, Boston, August 1978.

Waugh, N. C., & Norman, D. A. Primary memory. *Psychological Review*, 1965, *72*, 89–104.

Weiskrantz, L., & Warrington, E. K. Verbal learning and retention by amnesic patients using partial information. *Psychonomic Science*, 1970, *20*, 210–211. (a)

Weiskrantz, L., & Warrington, E. K. A study of forgetting in amnesic patients. *Neuropsychologia*, 1970, *8*, 281–288. (b)

Wernicke, C. Lehrbuch der Gehirnkrankheiten für Ärzte und Studierende. Berlin: Fischer, 1881.

Wickelgren, W. A. The long and short of memory. *Psychological Bulletin*, 1973, *80*, 425–438.

Wickelgren, W. A. Acoustic similarity and intrusion errors in short-term memory. *Journal of Experimental Psychology*, 1965, *70*, 102–108.

Wickens, D. D. Encoding categories of words: An empirical approach to meaning. *Psychological Review*, 1970, *77*, 1–15.

Winocur, G., & Kinsbourne, M. *Contextual cuing as an aid to Korsakoff amnesics*. Paper presented at the International Neuropsychological Society Meeting, Minneapolis, 1976.

Winocur, G., & Kinsbourne, M. Contextual cuing as an aid to Korsakoff amnesics. *Neuropsychologia*, 1978, *16*, 671–682.

Winocur, G., & Weiskrantz, L. An investigation of paired-associate learning in amnesic patients. *Neuropsychologia*, 1976, *14*, 97–110.

Witkin, H., Oltman, P. K., Raskin, E., & Karp, S. *A manual for the embedded figures tests*. Palo Alto, California: Consulting Psychologists Press, 1971.

Wood, F., & Kinsbourne, M. Paper in symposium on pathological forgetting. Paper presented at the International Neuropsychology Society Meeting, Boston, February 1974.

Woods, R., & Piercy, M. A similarity between amnesic memory and normal forgetting. *Neuropsychologia,* 1974, *12,* 437.

Subject Index

DATE DUE